Values and Ethics

Torah Topics for Today

By Fred and Joyce Claar

With Rabbi Moshe Becker,
Rabbi Diane Cohler-Esses,
Rabbi Gail Diamond,
Rabbi Judith Greenberg,
Rabbi Yael Hammerman,
Lois Kohn-Claar,
Rabbi Kerrith Rosenbaum,
Rabbi Charles E. Savenor

BEHRMAN HOUSE

www.behrmanhouse.com

This book is dedicated to Evan, Gary, Lois, Lilly, Ben, and Isaac

Content Creator/Editor/Writer: Fred Claar
Advisors/Editors: Joyce Claar, Lois Kohn-Claar
Line editor: Gail Diamond
Project editor: Dena Neusner
Design: Neustudio, Inc.
Production: Typeflow, Inc.

Published by Behrman House, Inc.
Millburn, New Jersey 07041
www.behrmanhouse.com

ISBN 978-0-87441-976-4
Printed in the United States of America

Names: Claar, Fred, author. | Claar, Joyce, author.
Title: Values and ethics : Torah topics for today / by Fred and Joyce Claar.
Description: New York : Behrman House, [2018] | Includes index. | Original
title: Values and ethics through a Jewish lens: talking points for family
discussion, published in Waccabuc, NY by Buoy Point Media, in 2015. |
"Grades 7 to 8 ; ages 11 and up."
Identifiers: LCCN 2017057378 | ISBN 9780874419764
Subjects: LCSH: Jewish ethics--Juvenile literature. | Bible. Old
Testament--Criticism, interpretation, etc.--Juvenile literature.
Classification: LCC BJ1285.2 .C53 2018 | DDC 296.3/6--dc23
LC record available at https://lccn.loc.gov/2017057378

CONTENTS

INTRODUCTION

The Torah is a guidebook for living. But how can a book that is more than three thousand years old speak to us today?

Maybe it is because basic human nature is very much the same today as in the past. From commandments about honoring our parents to stories of welcoming the stranger, the Torah is filled with values and ethics that we can learn from. It also provides stories of greed, anger, jealousy, and dishonesty. Torah study can help us learn the appropriate response to negative human traits, as well as teaching us to develop and cultivate positive ones.

Judaism has always emphasized education. It has survived for so long not by building monuments to itself, but by emphasizing the responsibility of parents and teachers to educate. We originally wrote *Values and Ethics: Torah Topics for Today* to empower parents to bring relevant values of Judaism into family discussions. Judaism practiced at home can have a positive long-term impact on the lives of families by transmitting values and traditions and by complementing the education that takes place in religious schools and community settings.

We have expanded the book to reach a wider audience of religious schools and youth groups, who can also benefit from the breadth and depth with which issues are developed here. Both teachers and parents can easily incorporate the lessons of *Values and Ethics* to bring Jewish values into the home, school, and community.

Themes of this book, such as jealousy, kindness, sibling rivalry, gratitude, anger, humility, and honesty, permeate the Torah. *Values and Ethics* shows us how to apply these themes and teachings to our lives today. Through the teachings and discussions in this book, you can join Jews all over the world and in Israel in studying the weekly Torah portion. It can be a thrilling concept to become part of a tradition of Torah study that has nurtured and inspired Jews for more than three thousand years.

In the Jewish tradition, the Torah is divided into fifty-four portions, with one read each week for a year. (Sometimes, to meet the exigencies of fitting the whole Torah into the yearly cycle, we read a double portion.) Congregations in synagogues around the world all read the same Torah portion each week. Thus Jews are connected to one another and to the annual cycle of weekly Torah portions, known as *parashat hashavua*.

This book follows this annual cycle of weekly Torah reading and provides two or three different ethical teachings for each Torah portion. To use this book, work it into your family rituals or ongoing classroom or youth group sessions. Read the brief passage that parallels the weekly Torah portion, or select a value of your choice from the subject index. Then discuss the questions that accompany each section with your class or family. Each page also contains an activity for active learning to help children and adults internalize and explore the message from the Torah portion. You can also visit our website www. valuesandethics.org to find material from *Values and Ethics* online.

INTRODUCTION *continued from page v*

New rituals can be hard to establish. Try repeating the weekly Torah study at least three times—even if it feels awkward at first—to give the practice a chance to become a natural part of your weekly activities. Even ten minutes of study a week will empower teachers, busy parents, and individuals to generate meaningful discussions about topics that touch the lives of everyone, regardless of their religious background or prior knowledge.

When we, Fred and Joyce, were young parents, we committed to modeling a Jewish life of values for our children. Friday nights were special family time to come together and share reflections on the week and to engage in meaningful conversations about life. These conversations helped us understand and be guided by the positive messages we discovered within the weekly Torah reading. Family and Shabbat guests valued these discussions, which continue today with our children and grandchildren at the Shabbat table.

We hope that this book makes a difference in your life and that you enjoy and find the same deep satisfaction from these discussions that we have.

Fred Claar
Joyce Claar

Values and Ethics

Torah Topics for Today

GENESIS

B'REISHIT בְּרֵאשִׁית

Torah Topics

When Rules Are Broken

> "You shall not eat
> of it or touch it."
>
> (Genesis 3:3)

Everyone breaks a rule at some time. How we deal with infractions is essential. Parents, teachers, and others in authority need to think about whether consequences are enforced with consistency.

The first book of the Bible, Genesis, has much to teach us about rule breaking. One of the first things God tells Adam is not to eat from the tree of knowledge. Yet the first story about Adam and Eve together is a story about their breaking this rule. Rule breaking seems to be part of who we are, part of what it means to be human.

Each time we break a rule presents an opportunity to take responsibility for our actions, whether or not there are immediate consequences. "Getting away with it" may give an initial high, which soon fades as guilt sets in. Telling the truth about what we did, examining why we crossed the line, and making amends to anyone we offended or harmed through our actions are important for moral development and future self-discipline.

—by Rabbi Dianne Cohler-Esses

MAKING CONNECTIONS

- Why do you think Adam and Eve broke their first rule?
- Which rules are the hardest for you to keep? Why?
- What kinds of rules do you find valuable? What kinds of rules do you find unfair?
- How can we resist the temptation to break a rule?

Rules

Take a list of rules that your group observes, such as classroom rules, youth group rules, or family rules. You may already have these rules written out, or you may need to write them. Write each on a small piece of paper, and put the papers in a hat. Ask each person to pick one and say why they find this rule important, or why they find it easy or difficult to observe. After everyone has had a turn, talk about what you learned in the discussion. This can be an opening to talk about general rules in society that you find helpful or difficult.

Sibling Rivalry

"Am I my brother's keeper?"
(Genesis 4:9)

Tension among brothers and sisters sometimes disrupts family harmony, causing bruised emotions that may last for months, even years. Feeling overshadowed because of the accomplishments of a sibling or feeling overlooked by parents may cause a family member to start a fight. How can we avoid these common family dilemmas?

Torah portion *B'reishit* includes the story of Cain and Abel, and humanity's first violent act: a lashing out of brother against brother based on jealousy and perceived favoritism. When Cain is asked, after he killed Abel, where his brother is, he replies, "Am I my brother's keeper?" (Genesis 4:9). The Torah is clearly teaching that the answer to Cain's question is *yes*.

What can families do to reduce jealousy and create positive family dynamics? Parents must recognize the special qualities of each child and help all family members appreciate the uniqueness of each person in the family. They need to balance praise with sensitivity to the feelings of other children. Children need to value their brothers and sisters as family and lifelong friends. It helps if the parents maintain good and caring relationships with their own siblings.

—*by Fred Claar*

....

MAKING CONNECTIONS

- What do you like about the way your family members get along with each other?
- What are some things that you would like to change?
- When do you get angry with your siblings and relatives? What do you do about it?
- Do you feel heard and appreciated in your family?
- What are some ways that you can show respect and appreciation for others in your family?

Role-play

Role-play the following situations of siblings who are different from one another: A sibling who is very athletic comes home with a prize, and his or her non-athletic sibling is home with the parents. What happens next? A sibling who has challenges in school comes home with an upsetting report card, and his or her straight-A-student sibling is home doing homework. What happens next? Two siblings are fighting over a tablet that one received as a present, and the parents walk in. What happens next? Act out these and other scenarios you make up. Look for ways to resolve situations with respect for one another.

Saying NO to Temptations

> "The serpent said to the woman, 'You are not going to die, but God knows that as soon as you eat of it your eyes will be opened and you will be like divine beings.'"
>
> (Genesis 3:4-5)

We are surrounded by things that tempt us. Unhealthy foods, video games, and gossip are just a few of the things enticing us. It's hard to make the decision to eat healthily, or to not play "just one more round," or to keep from spreading a juicy piece of news. When confronted with a temptation, we know what the right decision is, but in the moment, it can be so hard to stay connected to our values.

In this Torah portion, we have one of the most famous—and fateful—examples of someone giving in to temptation. In the Garden of Eden, God tells Adam not to eat from the tree of knowledge of good and bad. But the snake tempts Eve, and she and Adam eat from the tree. They give in to temptation because they see that the tree is appetizing and a source of wisdom.

When we give in to small temptations, our consequences might not be as grave as Adam and Eve's banishment from the Garden of Eden, but they also take a toll on us. We lose sight of what we value in favor of instant gratification. Not giving in to temptation helps us to clarify our values and stick to our convictions.

—*by Rabbi Judith Greenberg*

MAKING CONNECTIONS

- What are some things that tempt you, even though you know you should avoid them?
- Why is it sometimes hard to say no to temptations?
- What are some ways to avoid or overcome temptations?
- How does thinking long-range into the future help us to handle temptations?

The marshmallow test

Watch a video about "the marshmallow test," in which preschoolers are left alone with a marshmallow and told they will be rewarded if they can wait ten minutes and not eat it (the video can be found on YouTube). Discuss. Do you agree that this test would be a good predictor of success? Why is self-control an important quality to develop?

When Life Changes

"I am going to bring the Flood."
(Genesis 6:17)

Most families have to deal with difficult changes at some point or another—whether it's unemployment or illness or loss. Parents may have to help their children navigate the changes in their lives.

Noah, the hero of this Torah portion, experienced tremendous change. He and his family were the sole survivors of a flood that destroyed everything. They were forced to begin their lives all over again. But Noah, after all, wasn't perfect. After the Flood, one of the first things Noah did was to get drunk. By portraying Noah in this way, the Bible is acknowledging that it couldn't have been easy for Noah. The world changed dramatically for him, and he was forced to begin a new life. Beginning anew after loss can be arduous and lonely. Some people turn to drinking, overeating, or using drugs to help them through the rough spots, but surely abusing ourselves is not the answer.

Families going through changes need tools that offer alternatives to destructive behavior. Perhaps Noah didn't have the resources we might turn to—the support of friends, a peer group, or a religious community. Acknowledging the difficulty of the moment and accepting support can help both adults and children get through changes and back onto solid ground.

—by Rabbi Dianne Cohler-Esses

MAKING CONNECTIONS

- What have been difficult changes in your life?
- What has helped you deal with these changes?
- Have you or your family ever helped others who were going through difficult times? What did you do to help? How did you feel about it?

Resource map

Make a map of community services in your area that assist with food, housing, education, and other services. Where can families go for help in times of crisis? What agencies can help?

What Is Good Discipline?

> "The earth is filled with lawlessness."
> (Genesis 6:13)

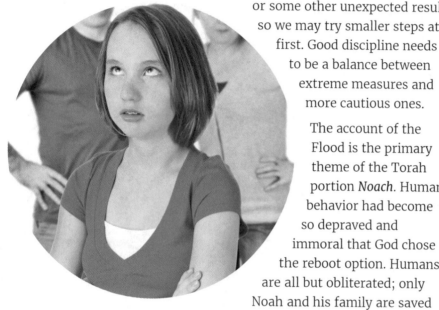

When a computer or smartphone misbehaves, it may need a reboot to get going again. At times that may be an extreme step. We may fear losing work or some other unexpected result, so we may try smaller steps at first. Good discipline needs to be a balance between extreme measures and more cautious ones.

The account of the Flood is the primary theme of the Torah portion *Noach*. Human behavior had become so depraved and immoral that God chose the reboot option. Humans are all but obliterated; only Noah and his family are saved to repopulate the earth. After the Flood, God indicates that this was an extreme option that will never be repeated. From this point forward God sets forth expectations of humanity with clear instructions and commandments on ways to live together properly for the benefit of all.

In our lives, bad behavior on our part can call for extreme or more cautious solutions. Extreme options might include changing schools, having to stay away from a friend who is a bad influence, or being restricted from certain activities. At other times, we respond to clear limits and expectations that help teach responsibility. After the Flood, God provides humanity with such rules and promises that the natural order of the world will never again be changed completely.

—by Rabbi Moshe Becker

MAKING CONNECTIONS

- Why do parents set limits on TV and electronics? What is the purpose of these limits?
- What would life be like if there were no rules and everyone could do exactly as he or she pleased?
- What rules can you think of that you would make if you were a parent?
- What would justify a major change in your life, such as changing schools?

Poster

Read about God's promises to Noah in Genesis 8:21–22 and 9:12–17. Work in small groups to make posters illustrating these themes.

"It Was a Dark and Stormy Night"

In the *Peanuts* comic strip, Snoopy begins each of his stories with the words "It was a dark and stormy night." Even if you're not a beagle living on top of a doghouse, life can often feel dark and stormy. Where do you go when you're having a tough day? To whom do you turn when you're having a bad night? We often turn to our families or closest friends to help us through the rough patches in life.

Like Snoopy, Noah has many dark and stormy nights. While it rains for forty days and nights and water floods the entire world, Noah's ark protects his family; his wife and children remain secure. They make it through the Flood safely and are able to start their lives again in peace.

Just as Noah and his family are protected from the Flood by their ark, we also have our own arks that guard us from the dark and stormy world. Our arks may be our families or our closest friends. We turn to them when we need support and protection. However, in order to make sure that our ark feels safe, we need to watch how we speak to one another and pay attention to how we handle our differences. Maintaining peace and security in our own families and friendships helps us keep the stormy world at bay.

—*by Rabbi Yael Hammerman*

> "The Flood continued forty days."
> (Genesis 7:17)

MAKING CONNECTIONS

- When has your life felt dark and stormy? To whom have you turned for help?
- Who are the people in your life who feel like an ark to you?
- How can families provide a safe space for each family member?

My room

Use a box and modeling clay to make a model of your room, either how it is or how you would like it to be. What can you put in your room to make it a safe place for you? Use your imagination to design the room of your dreams, or make a model of your room exactly as it is.

LECH L'CHA

Finding the Courage to Begin

"Adonai said to Abram, 'Go forth from your native land.'"
(Genesis 12:1)

New beginnings are hard, whether we are starting a new school, a new camp, or college. Before we embark on it, the journey is mysterious. We don't know what to expect. It can be frightening to leave the familiar and enter the unknown.

Abraham, in our Torah portion, is told to leave everything he knows—his family, his birthplace, and his home—and go to a place he does not know. Abraham has the courage to just go. There are no reports of him complaining or worrying. It is instructive for us to think about what enables Abraham to take this journey.

Abraham understands the limitations of the old and the possibilities of the new. Rather than focus on the frightening and unknown, he is able to imagine the positive possibilities of a new situation, and this gives him the strength to move forward. Likewise, we can imagine all the new friends we will make at a new school. Adults can envision the interesting challenges they will encounter at a new place of work. While new journeys can be intimidating, they can also be invigorating.

—by Rabbi Dianne Cohler-Esses

MAKING CONNECTIONS

- Think of something new in your life that has been scary for you. What was it?
- What helps you to have courage?
- What is the value of trying new places and activities?

Welcoming newcomers

Are there new people in your group, your synagogue, your community, or your school? Make some cookies, cards, or welcome baskets to give them. Talk about how you can welcome newcomers.

"The Grass Is Always Greener on the Other Side"

LECH L'CHA

Jealousy rears its ugly head when we least expect it. We may feel jealous of our friend's summer vacation plans, our brother's charisma, or our colleague's corner office. We may be envious of people we love and people we don't even know. We might resent a model's shiny hair, thin waist, and radiant smile or a singer's ability to hit an F-sharp. Envy fogs our ability to think straight and make good choices.

In this Torah reading, *Lech L'cha*, Sarah was jealous of her maid Hagar. Hagar easily became pregnant, while Sarah struggled to conceive. Resentment of Hagar's good fortune caused Sarah to treat Hagar harshly.

There will always be times when we find ourselves fueled by jealousy. However, we must realize that envy can lead us to make poor choices and treat others unfairly, as Sarah did. Moreover, jealousy can lead us to feel dissatisfied with our own lives so that we don't appreciate our own good fortune. We can try to examine the blessings in our own lives, rather than looking over someone else's shoulder and wanting what he or she has. When we feel jealous, we should remember that others may be jealous of us as well. If we try to stand in their shoes, we can better appreciate all the wonderful things we have in our lives.

—by Rabbi Yael Hammerman

> "Then Sarai treated her [Hagar] harshly, and she ran away from her."
>
> (Genesis 16:6)

MAKING CONNECTIONS

- When have you been jealous of others?
- Why would someone feel jealous of you?
- How can you remember your own good fortune when you feel envious of others?

Describing jealousy

Shakespeare called jealousy the "green-eyed monster." Why is the color green associated with envy? How do you feel when you are jealous? Work together on a list of descriptions of how jealousy feels.

9

LECH L'CHA

Choose Harmony

"Let there be no strife between you and me."
(Genesis 13:8)

Do you know any brothers and sisters who never argue? All siblings argue and usually each person arguing thinks he or she is correct and not at fault. Because fighting within a family is very common, our efforts have to focus everyone on the importance of living in peace. Disagreements will happen, but that doesn't mean that acrimony must prevail.

In this Torah portion, *Lech L'cha*, Abraham feels forced to ask his nephew Lot to part ways. Lot had accompanied Abraham through many of his travels, but staying together has become too difficult because their shepherds are constantly fighting. Abraham realizes that the disagreement is bound to continue, as each side is very sure of its position. Instead of allowing matters to deteriorate, Abraham chooses to put distance between himself and Lot. His goal is to preserve the harmony between them.

Separation is an extreme solution to a problem that can be handled by being willing to try to understand others. We can make that choice even when we think (or know) that the other person is wrong. Whether with a classmate, friend, or family member, there is almost always a way to maintain harmony in the face of different views, even if the solution is to agree to disagree. With creative thinking, humility, and acceptance, useless fighting can be avoided.

—by Rabbi Moshe Becker

MAKING CONNECTIONS

- Give an example of a fight that you could have avoided.
- What compromises can you think of that would have prevented ongoing fighting?
- Is it better to be right or to be loving?

Poster

Make a poster together of helpful words or expressions you can use to de-escalate an argument. For example, you might include statements like "I've never thought of it that way," "Maybe you're right," "Can we take a few minutes to cool off and talk about this later?" Use different colors to categorize the expressions as examples of humility, understanding, acceptance, and/or creative thinking.

Welcoming Guests into Your Home

Hospitality is a powerful way to model kindness. Opening our homes to others is a way to share with them the uniqueness of who we are and the blessings we have.

In this Torah portion, Abraham shows what an essential value hospitality is in the Bible. Surprisingly, even though he is in the midst of a conversation with God, he interrupts it to welcome three strangers he sees from afar. He begs them to stay awhile and have a morsel of bread and some water. Meanwhile, he and Sarah prepare a sumptuous meal for them. Abraham promises little but delivers much. He is a humble yet generous host.

Being humble and grateful for our blessings can make guests feel comfortable in our homes and go a long way toward forming and deepening friendships. Just as Abraham modeled exceptional behavior for us to follow, so too we can model kindness and generosity of spirit through hospitality.

—*by Rabbi Dianne Cohler-Esses*

> "He ran from the entrance of the tent to greet them."
> (Genesis 18:2)

MAKING CONNECTIONS

- When your friends are in your home, what are some of the special ways you should treat them?
- Why do you think it's important to treat guests well?
- When have you opened your home to family or to friends traveling or in need? Do you have regular events you host in your home?

Hosting

Host a meal or get-together. Depending on the nature and size of your group, you can invite another youth group chapter, a class, or a family to your home, school, or synagogue. Set a date for the event, and make plans to make your guests feel welcome. Discuss menus and other ways to ensure successful hosting.

VAYEIRA

Being Absolutely Honest

*"Sarah lied, saying,
'I did not laugh.'"*
(Genesis 18:15)

Is it ever okay not to tell the truth? What if someone asks you if a new outfit looks good and you think it looks bad? Should you say, "It doesn't look good on you," or should you say, "You look great"?

It's important to be honest, and to earn the trust of others. But ethically, there may be a time when it is okay to lie: when the truth will hurt someone for no good reason.

In this Torah portion, Sarah, when she hears that she will bear children, says to herself, "Now that I am withered, am I to have enjoyment—with my husband so old?" God amends Sarah's comment when God repeats it to Abraham, telling him that she said, "Shall I in truth bear a child, old as I am?" (Genesis 18:12–13). The tradition understands that God's change, leaving out the part about her husband being so old, was done in order to avoid hurting Abraham.

So, where does that leave us? These are issues of moral complexity. Sometimes people do lie or omit the truth for the sake of a greater good, such as sparing someone's feelings or maintaining peace. But this ethic can be dangerous. We must be careful not to justify lying when we lack the courage the hard truth requires.

—by Rabbi Dianne Cohler-Esses

....

MAKING CONNECTIONS

- Why is lying destructive to all concerned?
- Is it ever acceptable not to tell the truth? If so, when?
- Would it be acceptable to lie if you or someone with you were being threatened?

Play Two Truths and a Lie

Pass out index cards to each person. Everyone writes down two true statements about themselves and one lie; they then read their card or someone else's. Everyone has to guess which statement is the lie. After the game is over, remind participants that this is a game that works because we know the difference between truth and lies. Discuss the consequences of lying in other settings (on a resume, in a job interview, etc.).

Avoiding Hurting Words

We use words to express so many different aspects of ourselves: from basic needs like "I'm hungry" to sentiments like "I love you." Words have power to do good, but it is easy to forget how much harm we can do with them. We often think that our words cannot be hurtful if the person we are speaking about is not around, but with the prevalence of e-mail, texting, and Twitter, seldom do our words end when we first express them. It is safe to assume that any words we express will be heard or seen again.

In this Torah portion, *Vayeira*, Sarah speaks words that could be hurtful to Abraham. Thinking he cannot hear, she laughs about her husband's ability to father a child in his old age. Imagine how Abraham might have felt if he had heard Sarah's laughter. Later, in speaking to Abraham, God rephrases Sarah's words so as not to hurt Abraham's feelings. The Torah is teaching us to avoid hurtful speech.

How often do we speak carelessly and hurt those we love? We learn from this Torah portion that being in a relationship requires using our words to heal, whether we have been hurt or we have hurt someone else. Pausing to take a deep breath and counting to ten helps us to rephrase or avoid hurtful words. *Sh'lom bayit*, "peace in the home," is the responsibility of each family member.

—*by Rabbi Judith Greenberg*

"Am I to have enjoyment—with my husband so old?"
(Genesis 18:12)

MAKING CONNECTIONS

- What can you do to avoid saying words that hurt others?
- What are words that you can say after you have hurt someone?
- What is a good way to express your feelings when you have been hurt by someone else's words?

Word sculpture

Choose a special, positive word that has meaning for you (love, joy, hope, or any other word, in Hebrew or English). Use modeling clay or cookie dough to make a word sculpture or cookie in the shape of that word.

Choosing to Do Chores

> "She [Rebecca] ran back to the well to draw [water], and she drew for all his camels."
>
> (Genesis 24:20)

Chores can be hard when we are forced to do them, or easy and enjoyable if we choose to do them. What makes us willingly accept chores as our responsibilities, without having to be nagged or forced to do them?

This Torah portion offers some clues. We meet Rebecca, who is a picture of motion and energy. She is a young woman with a jug on her shoulder on her way to the well to draw water for her family. That was hard work due to the weight of the clay jug filled with water. Rebecca knows how important this chore of drawing life-sustaining water is to her family. She appears very willing to complete the task. Abraham's servant has been sent to look for a wife for Isaac. As soon as Rebecca sees him, she runs to fill her jug and gives him water, and then she runs back again to get water for his camels. Rebecca doesn't hesitate to be helpful. Not only does she fulfill her own obligations, but she goes beyond to help others and then their animals. Because of these qualities, Abraham's servant realizes that she will make an excellent wife for Isaac.

We can learn from Rebecca. She doesn't resist chores, because she knows that the responsibility for her family doesn't lie only with her parents. That responsibility is shared among adults and children alike. Everyone in a family needs to be committed to the well-being of the family. As we grow older, our responsibilities expand so that we are able to play a larger role in taking care of our families.

—by Rabbi Dianne Cohler-Esses

MAKING CONNECTIONS

- Which chores are easy for you? Which are hard? Why?
- What makes you like doing chores more?
- Studies show that kids who had to do chores are happier as adults. Why do you think that is?

Clean-up

Plan a clean-up activity you can do as a group inside your synagogue or classroom or at a nearby park. The activity should take at least one hour and involve the whole group. Afterward, reflect on what you accomplished and how you feel about completing the activity.

Reconciliation and Forgiveness

Obviously, people are not all the same. We are different from one another in many ways—how neatly we keep our rooms, what we eat, and the activities we like, for instance. It's easy to dwell on the differences, but there are also many core similarities that we share, and we need to focus on them.

Isaac and Ishmael are Abraham's two sons, half-brothers from different mothers. They are very different in age, temperament, experiences, mannerisms, and character. Yet this Torah portion, *Chayei Sarah*, emphasizes that when the time comes to bury and mourn their father Abraham, Isaac and Ishmael do so together. Isaac and Ishmael are able to set aside their differences to focus on what unites them.

Can we set aside our differences for the common good? Not everyone can or should be the same, and we may disagree with the way others behave or with their beliefs. But we all have much in common. We can focus on what unites us, such as family, values, community, and interests, and, like Isaac and Ishmael, seek ways to work together in harmony.

—by Rabbi Moshe Becker

> "Isaac and Ishmael buried him [Abraham] in the cave of Machpelah."
> (Genesis 25:9)

MAKING CONNECTIONS

- Give an example of an insignificant difference between you and a friend or family member.
- Give an example of a major difference between you and a friend or family member.
- What do you have in common with that person and how can you work together?
- Why is this important?

Web of connections

Stand in a circle with a ball of twine or yarn. One person starts, throwing the ball to someone they have something in common with and calling out the connection. It may be an item of clothing, the neighborhood you live in, a family name—anything that they share with the other person. Continue until everyone has been included and you have made a web of connections. Talk about what you found in common.

CHAYEI SARAH

Honoring Parents

"Then Laban [Rebecca's brother] and Bethuel [her father] answered [Eliezer]."
(Genesis 24:50)

In all likelihood, we have been taught to honor our parents. It's one of those Torah commandments that parents like. Parents may expect children to listen to and do everything they say. In truth, though, honoring parents should not entail giving up one's own life and dreams.

In this Torah portion, Abraham's trusted servant Eliezer approaches Rebecca's father, asking for permission to bring her back as a wife for Abraham's son Isaac. Laban, Rebecca's brother, in utter disrespect of his father, jumps up and responds before his father can speak.

We are not commanded to love our parents. The Torah is very free with the word "love," commanding us to love the stranger, love our neighbor, and love God; however, the Torah had the brilliance to recognize possible difficulties some may have with their parents. Therefore, the commandment is to honor our parents. We can learn how to express our opinions in a respectful way, whether or not we agree with our parents or elders. We must look out for our parents' needs with the same sense of responsibility they had when they cared for us.

—by Rabbi Moshe Becker

MAKING CONNECTIONS

- Why honor your parents?
- Can you name some opportunities to show honor to your parents?
- When we are angry with our parents, how should we behave toward them?

Song

Play a song about parents and children. Some suggestions: Cat Stevens, "Father and Son"; Elton John, "Blessed"; Crosby, Stills, Nash & Young, "Teach Your Children"; Will Smith, "Just the Two of Us"; or Ben Folds, "Gracie" (all available on YouTube). Ask participants to journal or share their thoughts about the song and honoring parents and children.

When Siblings Fight

Sibling rivalry occurs in all families with more than one child. It can, in some cases, be an insidious problem, and many families are at a loss for how to deal with it.

In our Torah portion, sibling rivalry threatens to become a lethal drama. Esau, as the eldest son of Isaac and Rebecca, stands to receive the preferred blessing of the eldest. However, Jacob, with his mother's help, presents himself to his dim-eyed father pretending to be Esau. Isaac gives Jacob the blessing reserved for the eldest, believing he is Esau. When Esau discovers this terrible deception, he says with a heart-rending cry, "Have you but one blessing, Father?" (Genesis 27:38). At first, Isaac refuses to bless Esau, saying that the blessing has already been spent on Jacob, but then he relents and blesses Esau also. Yet Esau seethes with resentment toward his brother. Jacob runs away from home to escape his brother's wrath, never to see his parents again.

Most sibling problems do not reach these mythic proportions. Yet even on a more limited scale, they can be pretty intense. Maybe there is something we can learn from the extreme example the Torah offers us. The key is in Esau's words, "Have you but one blessing, Father?" Each parent has many blessings to offer, and each child needs different kinds of blessing from his or her parents. Focusing on what each child needs rather than on fairness can take the edge off competition between siblings. Parents' love is an endless blessing, received differently by each child.

—*by Rabbi Dianne Cohler-Esses*

"Your brother came with guile and took away your blessing."
(Genesis 27:35)

MAKING CONNECTIONS

- If you have siblings, do you ever feel that things are unfair between you and them? Why or why not?
- Do you feel that your place in the family birth order (first, middle, last) has put you at an advantage or disadvantage? Why?
- Are there any positive sides to sibling rivalry?

Games day

Bring in your favorite family games. Share games and teach new games. Talk about how competition can be fun and healthy. How can we distinguish healthy from unhealthy rivalry?

Waiting for the Cookie to Cool

TOLDOT

> "Give me some of that red stuff to gulp down, for I am famished."
>
> (Genesis 25:30)

The sweet scent of freshly baked chocolate chip cookies wafts through the kitchen. Your mouth waters as you pull the hot tray out of the oven. The recipe says to let them cool for thirty minutes. But how can you wait when the cookies are calling your name?! You pick one up, but it crumbles and you burn your finger. You put the crumbs in your mouth and burn your tongue. This incident teaches us that we can't always get what we want right when we want it. There are many things in life that are well worth waiting for.

In Torah portion *Toldot*, Esau comes in from the field ravenous and begs Jacob for some lentil stew. Jacob agrees, but only if Esau promises to sell his birthright. Esau trades his inheritance for one meager meal of stew because he thinks with his stomach, acting on his animal instincts. If Esau had been patient, he most likely would have made a different decision.

This story teaches us the importance of delaying gratification. While it may not feel good to put some of your allowance in your piggy bank each week, it will feel great when you have finally saved enough money to buy a new bike. It might be painful to run sprints each morning or do endless sets of soccer drills, but it feels glorious when you cross the finish line or score the winning goal.

—by Rabbi Yael Hammerman

MAKING CONNECTIONS

- Think of a time you let your stomach make a decision for you that you later regretted or a time you acted on an impulse instead of thinking through a decision more carefully. How do you feel looking back on these experiences?

- Have you ever worked really hard to achieve a goal? How did it feel when you accomplished the goal?

Gardening

If you have the opportunity, plant spring flower bulbs in the fall. Or plant parsley seeds and then harvest the parsley for the Pesach seder. Or visit a community garden. Talk about the growing cycle and how long you have to wait to see the flowers or eat the parsley. How can you implement the principles we learn from tending plants into your life?

Breaking the Cycle of Deceit

Nothing gets attention at summer camp like pulling a good prank. The pranks start out small. First the boys' bunk toilet-papers the girls' cabin. The girls retaliate by short-sheeting the boys' beds. The boys hit back by putting the girls' luggage in the dumpster; then the boys find their sleeping bags filled with shaving cream. Before you know it, a full-blown prank war spirals out of control. No one is safe from the practical jokes—or from the camp director's punishment. What began as a small act of trickery quickly erupts into a serious situation with consequences.

In this Torah reading, *Toldot*, Jacob pulls the ultimate prank on his father Isaac. He pretends to be his twin brother Esau in order to receive the blessing reserved for Isaac's first-born son. Though Jacob later flees from his father's house, he cannot escape his deceitful act. Later, Jacob himself is deceived in turn by his father-in-law, Laban, just as he fooled his own father.

Jacob could not escape from his history of trickery. Similarly, our misdeeds follow us in unimaginable ways as well. It can be hard to break a cycle of deception and pranks. However, before we experience serious consequences, we must find different ways to relate to others.

—*by Rabbi Yael Hammerman*

> "Jacob said to his father, 'I am Esau, your first-born.'"
> (Genesis 27:19)

MAKING CONNECTIONS

- Have you ever pulled a prank or been pranked? What was it like pulling a prank? What was it like being on the receiving end?
- How can we tell the difference between a "harmless prank" and something more serious?
- Have you ever deceived anyone or been deceived? How did it feel?
- Have your actions ever come back to haunt you?

Pretending to be someone else

Pair up with a partner. Talk to your partner for a few minutes about yourself, or your day, or anything that comes to mind, while your partner observes you carefully. Then your partner should pretend to be you for a few minutes. Then switch. How does it feel to pretend to be someone else? How would you have felt if you were Jacob pretending to be Esau?

How Can We Improve?

> "A stairway was set on the ground and its top reached to the sky."
>
> (Genesis 28:12)

We all plan projects for self-improvement. One mistake we often make, however, is that we think we can change ourselves all at once. The truth is that changing one's self doesn't happen easily. It happens slowly and by increments.

In this Torah portion, Jacob leaves home and a difficult family situation. He lies down to sleep and has a spectacular dream. He dreams of angels going up and down a ladder, step-by-step. The dream might signify that Jacob can only progress in his journey step-by-step. Jacob is a model for us, showing that we too can make progress only step-by-step.

When trying to improve our character, we cannot leap up quickly. Small steps "up the ladder" can lead to large accomplishments over time. Quick leaps, on the other hand, can lead to falling down the ladder. To be secure, a ladder needs to lean against something high up. It is to be expected that we may slip back a rung, but we should not worry. We can catch hold of the next rung and start climbing again. Lasting change is never achieved quickly or easily. To reach our personal goals, we need to keep climbing, like Jacob, one step at a time.

—by Rabbi Dianne Cohler-Esses

MAKING CONNECTIONS

- What would you like to change about yourself?
- How would you go about doing that?
- What do you think would be easy to change? What would be difficult to change?

Mussar journal

Mussar is a Jewish practice that encourages self-improvement. For this exercise, get a small notebook and start a journal. On the first page, write something about yourself that you would like to change. Then every day, write a little bit, even just one sentence, about what happened relative to your goal and how you see yourself changing or staying the same. Keep this up for at least one month, and report to the group about what you learn and what happens.

Dealing with Dishonesty

There are times when we deny the truth, especially when accused. When Adam was accused by God of eating the apple, he blamed it on Eve, and she blamed it on the snake. It's difficult to confront people directly with the truth when we know they are lying. It can be easier to ignore the dishonesty rather than confront the dishonest person.

We can take a lesson from our patriarch Jacob in this Torah portion, *Vayeitzei*. Laban, his father-in-law, tricks Jacob by giving him Leah as a wife, when her younger sister Rachel had been promised. Much later, Jacob says to him, "Of the twenty years that I spent in your household, I served you fourteen years for your two daughters, and six years for your flocks; and you changed my wages ten times" (Genesis 31:41). After twenty years of living under the thumb of his father-in-law, Jacob courageously confronts him directly with the truth.

We can communicate the importance of honesty by being honest ourselves and calling others on their dishonesty. Silence and lies can be very destructive to relationships, causing us to present a false self to the world. Therefore we must strive to be as courageous and honest as possible in our day-to-day dealings.

—*by Rabbi Dianne Cohler-Esses*

> "Your father has cheated me, changing my wages time and again."
> (Genesis 31:7)

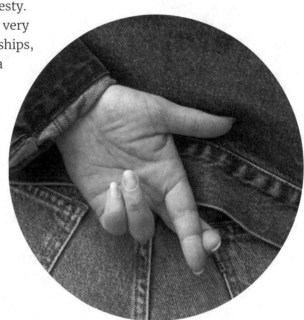

MAKING CONNECTIONS

- Did you ever catch yourself or someone else lying? How did you feel? How did you respond?
- In what other ways could you have responded?

Role-play

Role-play the following situations in which a person wants to conceal information but not to lie: Someone just came from the doctor but doesn't want their friend to know where they were. Someone whose parents are divorced doesn't want to say so to a new classmate. Someone is really hungry because there is no food in their house for breakfast. How does it feel to try to conceal information? How can we handle these kinds of situations?

Tithing

"Of all that You give me, I will set aside a tithe for You."
(Genesis 28:22)

We all have something to give. By giving, we show that we are responsible for those less fortunate in our communities and, more broadly, in the world. We can give financially. Even a child can set aside a small part of his or her allowance. We can also give by volunteering our time. Especially when we feel things are missing in our own lives, helping others can help us realize how we are blessed in different ways.

In this Torah portion, *Vayeitzei*, Jacob promises to give a tenth of everything he receives. At this point, he has nothing. He has just run away from home and left everything behind. Having no idea what is before him, he makes this promise. If he remains poor, a tenth would be a small gift, but a dear sacrifice. If he grows wealthy, a tenth would be a much larger gift, but perhaps easier to part with. Jacob promises that whatever comes his way, he will give a tenth of it.

Giving to those less fortunate than ourselves can help us recognize the great blessings in our lives. It reminds us that we cannot take credit for the richness we receive. Just as Jacob did not know what was before him, we do not know what the future will bring for us. But, like Jacob, we should not wait for a better day to help others; we should commit to help today and every day.

—by Rabbi Judith Greenberg

MAKING CONNECTIONS

- In what ways do you feel blessed?
- Who in your community needs your help? Who in the broader global community?
- How does it feel to give to those less fortunate than you?
- Does giving of our time bring a different kind of satisfaction from giving money or objects?

Tzedakah boxes

Make and decorate tzedakah boxes (you can find directions for making them using recycled materials online). Set a date for an "allocations meeting" when everyone will return the boxes and decide how to allocate the funds together.

How to Wrestle with Inner Struggles

We all struggle. Children, teens, and adults often struggle to control intense and contradictory emotions. At different life stages, wrestling can be particularly intense. School, future plans, and family pressures can all present challenges.

In this Torah portion, Jacob struggles mightily. Alone in the middle of the night, separated from his family and possessions, he encounters a stranger. Commentators say it is a divine messenger. Jacob and the stranger wrestle until dawn. The stranger, before leaving, gives Jacob a new name, Israel, which means "one who struggles with God," and then blesses him.

The people who are descended from Jacob/Israel are called by his name.

This story illustrates that struggle can lead to change and personal growth. Everyone has struggles, and struggles help us grow.

—by Rabbi Dianne Cohler-Esses

> "A man wrestled with him [Jacob] until the break of dawn."
>
> (Genesis 32:25)

MAKING CONNECTIONS

- What do you struggle with?
- What helps you in your struggles?
- How can family and friends support you in your struggles?

Challenge course

Take a trip to an adventure challenge course, climbing wall, or playground, or make your own obstacle course. If the course is easy, time all participants and then encourage them to beat their best time. Talk about what you learned about yourselves by conquering a physical challenge. How can you apply what you learned today to other aspects of your life?

Being Content with What You Have

> "Esau said, 'I have enough, my brother.'"
> (Genesis 33:9)

We each have our own methods for calculating happiness, criteria that we think are important when judging our level of comfort. While it is often easy to list all that we wish we had, sometimes it is harder to take stock of what we already have. Sometimes we need a reminder to be appreciative and give proper value to what we may take for granted.

This Torah portion, *Vayishlach*, contains the story of two brothers, Jacob and Esau. At one point in the story, Esau expresses to Jacob that he has enough and that Jacob should keep what is his so that he too can have enough. This shows a great deal of self-awareness on Esau's part. Not only is he content with his portion, but he wants others to recognize their own bounty as well.

In the Ethics of the Fathers (*Pirkei Avot*) we learn, "Who is rich? The one who appreciates what he has." While this seems like such simple advice, in this age of plenty we often struggle to follow it. First we have to be aware enough to recognize what we have, and only then can we be truly appreciative of it. As we become better at doing this for ourselves, we can also help others to recognize their own good fortune.

—by Rabbi Kerrith Rosenbaum

MAKING CONNECTIONS

- What aspects of your life do you appreciate?
- How do you show your appreciation?
- What are some things that you wish were different and why?
- In what ways can you work with those feelings while still being thankful for what you have?

Make an inventory

On one side of a page, make a list of every single object in your room (from memory). Turn the paper over and make a list of intangible things that you have in your life, such as friends, family, community, health, and so on. Make both lists as long as you can. Now share them with a partner. How do you feel about what's on your lists? See if you can write a poem or draw a picture that expresses how you feel.

"Israel" Means "Struggle with God"

VAYISHLACH

"Your name shall no longer be Jacob, but Israel."
(Genesis 32:29)

Many people hold back on religion in their lives because they are uncomfortable with the concept of God. Does God exist? If so, why do bad things happen to good people? Why does evil exist? These are all questions that people have addressed throughout time. Many sophisticated discussions and answers are embedded in Jewish texts that we encounter and wrestle with personally.

In this Torah portion, *Vayishlach*, Jacob wrestles all night with a mysterious angel representing God. Because Jacob successfully survives this encounter, his name is changed to Israel, which means "struggle with God" in Hebrew. The Torah is saying that to struggle with God is common.

We may struggle with our conception of God, questioning and studying throughout our lives to come to terms with our own personal encounter with God. We are not asked to accept faith in God blindly, but to question, to study the wisdom of our sages, to do good works, and to seek to encounter God within ourselves.

—*by Fred Claar*

MAKING CONNECTIONS

- What clues might we find in life or nature to God's existence?
- What are some questions you have about God?
- How do your questions about God affect your view of religion?
- How might you begin your personal journey to wrestle with God?
- How could a journey in life be more important than the destination?

Painting

Numerous artists have explored their conceptions of God by painting the scene of Jacob wrestling with the angel. View some of their artworks online, and then use watercolors or poster paints to depict your own vision of wrestling with God or of Jacob's encounter.

VAYEISHEV

Caring for One Another: Building an Eternal Bond

"Israel loved Joseph best of all his sons."
(Genesis 37:3)

Brothers and sisters sometimes act in a caring manner and sometimes don't. Sometimes they tell on one another, and sometimes they defend each other. To keep our families connected into future generations, we need a family culture where brothers and sisters care deeply about each other.

In this Torah portion, there is tremendous strife between Joseph and his brothers. Jacob, their father, clearly plays favorites and gives Joseph a multicolored coat to signify his love for Joseph. Joseph fuels the tension created by this favoritism by telling on his brothers.

It may sometimes seem that parents favor one child over another, especially if one child is effortlessly successful while other siblings have a more difficult time achieving. People flourish and feel loved when the focus is on each individual's uniqueness and achievements. While siblings cannot help but compare themselves to one another, the more they feel loved for who they are, the more they will thrive and be able to care genuinely for each other.

—by Rabbi Dianne Cohler-Esses

MAKING CONNECTIONS

- Do you have siblings? If so, what do you like best about them? If not, do you have rivalry with any friends or relatives?
- What helps siblings get along?
- In what ways do you feel your own talents and unique qualities are appreciated or not appreciated?

Trading card

Make your own collectible trading card with your picture (real or drawn) showing your special talents and superpowers. You can also make cards for siblings or family members, focusing on their positive qualities. Make a display of all the cards your group makes.

The Light at the End of the Tunnel

Have you ever been pushed to go to an event that you did not want to attend and then had a great time? Did you ever start out disliking a very demanding teacher and later in the year appreciate that teacher for making you a much better student? Many times in life things are not what they seem to be at first.

This Torah portion, *Vayeishev*, contains one of the most famous examples of how something that starts off badly comes to a good end. Joseph, the favored youngest son of Jacob, is sold into slavery by his jealous brothers. He seems destined for a life of enslavement in Egypt when a turn of fortune brings him into the good graces of Pharaoh. Joseph's life quickly changes as he rises to the top of Egyptian society, gaining fame, security, and fortune. This is a very positive end to a dreadful beginning.

Sometimes we simply need to look a little harder to find the good in what feels bad. Often we need patience to wait for changes. It can be hard to hold out hope when things feel as though they are not going our way, but a positive outlook on the world can go a long way toward making situations feel more manageable. Being able to look forward and see a "light at the end of the tunnel" can help make the journey easier.

—by Rabbi Kerrith Rosenbaum

"Come, let us sell him to the Ishmaelites."
(Genesis 37:27)

MAKING CONNECTIONS

- Can you describe a time in your life when events had an unexpected outcome?
- How do you feel when events don't turn out the way you expect?
- How do you cope when things are not going your way?

Guest speaker

Invite the child of a Holocaust survivor, a Jew who lived in the Soviet Union, or a refugee to visit your group and tell his or her story. Discuss how the speaker's life may have changed in unexpected ways.

VAYEISHEV

"My son's tunic!
A savage beast
devoured him!"
(Genesis 37:33)

Being Honest

Words have power. They can lift someone's spirits, but they can also cause damage. Words can sometimes be smokescreens for what is truly taking place, or they can be used as defenses from shame and pain. It is natural to want to please parents, teachers, and friends. However, when mistakes and errors in judgment arise, some people go to great lengths to shield themselves from punishment and embarrassment, including lying. It is easy to forget that words of truth and transparency are building blocks of loving, secure relationships.

The story of Joseph and his brothers is a cautionary tale of parenting and brotherhood. All Jacob's sons desire is their father's affection, the kind of attention that Joseph receives. Yet the more Jacob favors Joseph, the more his other sons resent their brother. Was Jacob aware of how his special attention to Joseph affected his other children? The brothers act out their anger against Joseph by selling him as a slave. Then they betray their father's trust by leading him to believe that Joseph has been eaten by a wild animal. Instead of owning up to their mistakes, Jacob's sons attempt to save face. Rather than speaking openly at the outset about their needs, the brothers end up breaking their father's heart.

We don't always know how to express our needs, including our desire for attention and affection. We may even tell tall tales or act out in order to get people to notice us. A better way to behave is by being honest and using words to create clarity and stronger relationships.

—by Rabbi Charles E. Savenor

MAKING CONNECTIONS

- Have you ever withheld the truth to avoid getting into trouble? How did that make you feel?
- Is there a difference between telling a lie and withholding information? If so, what is it?
- How do you tell your parents that you need them?

Telling the truth

Make a list of subjects or situations in which it's hard to tell the truth. Then take turns acting out the situations and being the person who has to tell a difficult truth.

Growth through Forgiveness: Reconciliation, Not Revenge

All families experience strife at some point. There may be a distancing of siblings, a child angry at a parent, or a parent angry at a child. It's important to move past this angry distancing toward reconciliation.

In this Torah portion, Joseph takes revenge on his brothers for throwing him into a pit and selling him into slavery. It's no wonder. His pain was sufficient to make anyone want to take revenge. When his brothers travel to Egypt to obtain grain for their family in the face of a famine, they have no idea that the powerful man who stands before them dispensing grain is none other than Joseph himself. Joseph takes advantage of his secret identity and throws Judah into jail and then threatens to enslave Benjamin. In the next Torah portion, Judah courageously approaches Joseph. He makes it clear that if he and his brothers don't return home with Benjamin, his father will be grievously hurt. Joseph is overcome with emotion. "I am your brother Joseph," he says, "he whom you sold into Egypt" (Genesis 45:4). Joseph and his brothers have an emotional reconciliation, and Joseph weeps and embraces his brothers.

Judah's courage in approaching Joseph allows Joseph to move away from revenge toward reconciliation. That powerful but simple caring gesture reaches underneath Joseph's rage and leads him to reveal his identity. We, like Judah, can approach the other, and like Joseph we can forgive when our anger has cooled down.

—*by Rabbi Dianne Cohler-Esses*

> "Joseph's brothers came and bowed low to him."
> (Genesis 42:6)

MAKING CONNECTIONS

- What is the best way to approach another family member after a fight?
- What can make it easier to reconcile?
- Why do you think it's important to forgive?

Bibliodrama

Act out the scene in which Joseph reveals himself to his brothers (Genesis 45:1–15). Have different people play the different roles and make up their own lines. Afterward, talk about what it felt like to be Joseph or his brothers and how it felt to reconcile.

Self–Esteem

> "Though Joseph recognized his brothers, they did not recognize him."
> (Genesis 42:8)

We naturally want life to be easy. We may be uncomfortable struggling with homework, and we may ask our parents for more help than we should. Deep down we know that when we complete the task ourselves, we feel better about ourselves and we learn a lot more, both about the material and our abilities.

Joseph is abducted and sold by his brothers into slavery. This Torah portion takes place years later when he has become viceroy to the king of Egypt and wields tremendous power. His brothers come to Egypt from Canaan to buy food for their families. As they approach Joseph, he recognizes them, but they do not know him. Instead of immediately revealing himself or punishing them, he puts them through a series of tests. He gives them the opportunity to show that they have learned to look out for each other and put differences aside. He allows them to redeem themselves in his eyes and to show concern for their father, Jacob.

Joseph chose the long route, providing an opportunity for his brothers to look at him, at their father, and at themselves once again. Sometimes we have to be willing to go through a slow process to learn. That means completing projects we have chosen or learning to resolve fights on our own. These are opportunities to work for success on our own, which we can feel proud of.

—by Rabbi Moshe Becker

MAKING CONNECTIONS

- Give an example of something you think you are good at doing.
- Give an example of something you know you could become better at doing.
- What is the difference between self-esteem and inflated ego?
- How do self-esteem and humbleness relate to each other?

Compliments

Sit in a circle. Each person has to give a compliment to the person on his or her left. The compliment should be on a social skill or quality (for example: I like how you listen well to others). The person receiving the compliment has to accept it by saying thank you without deflecting the compliment. Talk about how it feels to give and receive compliments.

Moving beyond Denial

Sometimes the truth is sitting right in front of us but we just can't see it. Luckily, we don't move through this world alone. We have friends, family, and teachers who can help us gain perspective on our own lives. We just need to learn to listen.

In this Torah portion, *Mikeitz*, Joseph's brothers are blinded by denial. They have come down to Egypt in search of food due to the famine in their own land. None of the eleven brothers can see that the Egyptian official in front of them is their brother, Joseph, whom they sold into slavery years ago, telling their father that he had died. Joseph tries to give them a hint by seating them in age order, an order only a family member would know. But they still do not understand what is going on.

It is not until Joseph, giving up on all subtleties, says to them, "I am your brother Joseph" (Genesis 45:4), that they realize who he is.

It took the shock of finding their long-lost brother to open their eyes to reality. Do we miss important clues in our own lives? Do we hold back from new challenges because we are in denial about our abilities to handle them? All of us can break out of denial into reality, but it is hard to do alone. We each have people in our own lives who can help us move away from unrealistic denial. Parents, teachers, brothers, and sisters are often able to help us see our own world in perspective. We just need to be open to them.

—by Rabbi Judith Greenberg

> "They were seated by his direction, from oldest . . . to the youngest."
> (Genesis 43:33)

MAKING CONNECTIONS

- When have you learned a lesson about yourself from a friend?
- What makes it hard to listen when someone is giving you advice?
- How can we learn to be more open?

Revealing secret messages

Use a white crayon to write a secret message or draw an invisible picture. Then trade your work with a partner. Paint over the page with watercolor paints to reveal the message. Did you learn something about your partner by revealing their hidden message? Could there be other hidden messages around? What might help us notice them?

VAYIGASH

Speaking Softly

> "Please, my lord, let
> your servant speak
> a word to my lord."
>
> (Genesis 44:18)

It can be easy to be impulsive and become angry or frustrated when things don't go our way. We may speak sharply or yell at those around us without thinking.

In this Torah portion, Joseph, who is unrecognizable to his brothers because he is dressed as Egyptian royalty, mistreats his brothers for having thrown him into a pit and plotted to sell him into slavery. He plants his silver goblet in his beloved brother Benjamin's sack, and once it is discovered, he declares that Benjamin will be his slave. Judah approaches him and says, "Please, my lord, let your servant speak a word to my lord. Do not be angry with your servant, though you are equal to Pharaoh himself" (Genesis 44:18).

Despite the difficult and tense situation, Judah approaches his brother with gentleness and speaks softly to him. Thus he defuses the tension in the situation. In response, Joseph breaks down and reveals his real identity to his brothers. By speaking softly at home, we show that shouting is not the most effective way. Gentleness can often be more productive than harsh yelling. The more we curb our own tendency to anger, the more we demonstrate that kindness can be the most effective way to behave.

—by Rabbi Dianne Cohler-Esses

MAKING CONNECTIONS

- How do you like to be treated?
- How do you feel when you are treated with less than kindness?
- Do you ever treat others meanly?

Sayings and slogans

Look up some quotes about kindness. Choose one that speaks to you, and make a poster of it to hang in your school, synagogue, or home. You can prepare for this activity ahead of time by bringing a sheet of quotations to choose from.

Not Embarrassing Others

Kids often embarrass other kids in front of friends, behavior that causes pain, shame, and hurt. Jewish tradition recognizes how painful humiliation can be, and it considers embarrassing someone in public very serious, comparable to killing someone.

In this Torah portion, Joseph provides a good model for us. Joseph has been estranged and separated from his brothers for years following his painful experience at their hands. He has become a powerful Egyptian ruler. After so many years, his brothers do not recognize Joseph, who is dressed as an Egyptian. It seems that after Judah pleads with Joseph not to imprison his younger brother Benjamin, Joseph forgives his brothers. He then demands that all the Egyptians leave the room. Only when left alone with his brothers does he reveal his identity. Not knowing how they will react, he protects their privacy by asking everyone outside the family to leave the room. Despite the harm his brothers have done him, Joseph is attuned to their feelings and does not want to embarrass them in front of others.

Joseph's sensitivity gives us a clue of how to behave in our own homes. By being more sensitive to potential embarrassment, we can show others how to be sensitive. Some simple guidelines can spare embarrassment: don't talk about other people; don't reveal other people's secrets; allow everyone privacy.

—by Rabbi Dianne Cohler-Esses

> "There was no one else about when Joseph made himself known to his brothers."
> (Genesis 45:1)

MAKING CONNECTIONS

- Have you ever been embarrassed publicly or seen someone else embarrassed? How did you handle the situation?
- Why do we sometimes embarrass people in front of others?
- What can we do to make sure we don't embarrass others publicly?

Brainstorming

Pair up and make a list of situations that you find embarrassing. Then brainstorm ways to respond to them. Ask each pair to report back some of their best methods for getting out of or surviving embarrassing situations.

Lying Does Not Pay

> "Joseph is still alive; yes, he is ruler over the whole land of Egypt."
> (Genesis 45:26)

Mistakes happen, and nobody likes to make mistakes. It is very tempting, and often convincing, to present and/or perceive the facts a bit differently. We may deny something we said or did, or we may convince ourselves that we didn't do anything wrong. This behavior is shortsighted.

Joseph was sold by his brothers because they decided they wanted to get rid of him. After selling Joseph, his brothers engaged in an elaborate deception designed to give their father the impression that Joseph had been torn apart by wild animals. Much to their shock, Joseph appears many years later as a ruler in Egypt. Now the brothers are faced with the very uncomfortable reality of being caught. Not only did they commit a crime against their brother, but they also lied to their father.

We rarely lie out of malice or a desire to be dishonest. More often than not, we end up lying because it's more convenient to invent an untruth than to admit to an uncomfortable truth. But if someone else sees or hears, we're in double trouble for what happened and for lying about it. This may damage their ability to trust us. We must remember to keep the long-term ramifications of a lie in mind.

—by Rabbi Moshe Becker

MAKING CONNECTIONS

- Why are we tempted to lie?
- Is it bad to lie or just not smart? Explain your answer.
- Is it ever right to lie? Why or why not?

Lying about qualifications

Multiple webpages and videos discuss the phenomenon of lying on college applications and resumes. Choose a video or article for your group to watch or read, and have an open discussion. What drives people to lie about their qualifications? Why is it a bad idea?

Each Family Has a Mission in the World

Each family has a mission in the world. For example, your family mission might be to become positive, contributing members of society, who have compassion for others and do good in the world. Everything we do as a family, large and small, contributes to our overall mission.

In this *parashah*, we find Jacob on his deathbed, offering a blessing to each of his sons. Each blessing includes a vision of that child's future. For example, when blessing Judah, Jacob blesses both Judah and Judah's descendants as leaders in Israel.

Parents needn't wait until they are dying to bless their children. Traditionally, Jewish parents give blessings to each of their children every Friday night. While there is a blessing from the Torah that many parents say, others make up their own blessings. What a wonderful practice it would be to bless members of your family each week and to make the mission of your family explicit in your blessings.

—by Rabbi Dianne Cohler-Esses

> "The scepter shall not depart from Judah, nor the ruler's staff."
>
> (Genesis 49:10)

MAKING CONNECTIONS

- What does it mean to you to bless another person?
- What would you like to bless your family with?
- Do we focus enough on the things our families are doing right?

Writing blessings

Write blessings to the members of your family. What do you wish for them now and in the future? You can write individual blessings or a blessing for your family as a whole. Decorate and share them with your family.

Family Forgiveness

> "Although you intended me harm, God intended it for good."
>
> (Genesis 50:20)

We've all been offended at one time or another by the words or actions of a family member. Parents, children, spouses, and siblings do end up hurting each other, willfully or unintentionally. When it comes to family, the ability to forgive is crucial. Family is meant to be permanent, and having the strength to forgive makes it possible for relationships to continue to grow and develop.

This Torah portion gives a very clear message on the importance of family forgiveness. In it we are reminded that years earlier, Joseph's brothers sold him into slavery and told their father that Joseph had been killed. Jacob, Joseph's father, was devastated, and Joseph became a slave in Egypt before ultimately rising to a position of power. Wisely, Joseph forgives all his brothers for their malicious acts, realizing that he and his brothers share a common identity and future that should not be jeopardized by grudges, even if they seem justified. Jacob also forgives his sons for their cruel deception. This is a powerful story with a very relevant message for life today.

The need to forgive and, if possible, forget, is vitally important. Calmly confront wrongdoers and explain what they have done as a step toward reconciliation, not increased hostility. When we consider how others forgive us, we realize we too benefit when we forgive others. How we treat our whole family is important. Forgiveness is an ability that is within our power.

—by Rabbi Moshe Becker

MAKING CONNECTIONS

- Why is it hard to forgive others?
- Why is holding a grudge ultimately damaging?
- What tools can we learn to reduce our pain at family hurts and insults?

Writing exercises

Option 1—Letters not to send: Write a letter to someone you are mad at. This letter is just for you, but write it as if you are writing to that person. Write down exactly what you are mad about. Then write what you wish could happen between you. *Option 2—Letters from Joseph to his brothers:* Write letters that Joseph might have sent to his brothers the week after he became a slave, the week after Pharaoh promoted him, and the week after he saw his brothers again. How do the letters change as the story unfolds?

Think before Acting

When we are angry, our vision narrows and we sometimes act in ways that would shock ourselves in a better moment. It is hard to maintain perspective when someone or something angers or offends us. But upon reflection, we are able to look back on our actions and make changes for the future.

In this Torah portion, *Vay'chi*, Jacob, from his deathbed, shares parting words with all of his sons. These are not the blessings you might expect from a dying patriarch. Many of them are quite critical. Jacob scolds his sons Reuben, Simeon, and Levi for their reckless behavior from years before, which includes sexual misconduct and a massacre. Years later, these sons are still dealing with the consequences of their actions. In the moment, when the brothers did these things, they surely did not consider these consequences. Imagine how they must feel upon realizing their father is still hurting from their actions, so many years later.

Slowly counting to ten can prevent us from yelling or making a mean remark, whether it be toward a loved one or a classmate. Rereading an impassioned e-mail or text message can help us press "delete" instead of "send." When we do take an action that we later regret, we can reflect on what led us to take that step in order to avoid doing it again. Thinking about those we have hurt in the past can help us be more careful in the future.

—by Rabbi Judith Greenberg

> "This is what their father said to them as he bade them farewell."
> (Genesis 49:28)

MAKING CONNECTIONS

- What do you do when you are angry?
- Can you think of a time when you stopped yourself from expressing anger? How did it feel?
- How can you communicate anger in a productive way?

Make an emotions wheel

Take a circular piece of white poster board or a paper plate and make lines to form eight pie sections. Label each section with a word for an emotion: anger, happiness, sadness, frustration, etc. Then color each section of the wheel in a different color. You can also make emoji decorations to show each emotion. The wheel helps remind us that emotions change and can help us to identify our emotions. Share your wheel with the group, and if you feel comfortable, share your ideas about how we can move from one emotion to another.

EXODUS
SH'MOT שְׁמוֹת

Torah Topics

When to Intervene

> "He found two Hebrews fighting; so he said to the offender, 'Why do you strike your fellow?'"
>
> (Exodus 2:13)

Sometimes we witness troubling events, at work or school or in public, and we wrestle with deciding whether to intervene. Is it "none of our business," or should we say something? Knowing which is which is challenging. If someone helpless is being demeaned, it's important to step in and help out. Otherwise, by not doing anything, we become accomplices to the problem. Whether to act discreetly or openly is a decision we will have to make in each situation.

In this Torah portion, which begins the second book of the Bible, Exodus, Moses grows up and begins to feel compassion for his people who are suffering in slavery. One day he sees two Hebrews fighting and confronts the one who started the conflict. He intervenes with a simple question: "Why do you strike your fellow?" (Exodus 2:13). This shows us that sometimes asking a question at the right moment can serve as a powerful intervention to protect someone.

Discussing troubling incidents with family and friends can be a learning experience to help guide us on how to behave in the future. Explaining your feelings and actions in a situation you face and hearing how others would handle or have dealt with similar circumstances can help to clarify the difference between minding your own business and knowing when and how to intervene. It is not an easy distinction to make, but it is important to look for ways to intervene successfully to stop harmful behavior.

—by Rabbi Dianne Cohler-Esses

MAKING CONNECTIONS

- Has anyone ever intervened for you in an uncomfortable or dangerous situation? Have you ever intervened?
- Have you ever seen a situation where you or others could have intervened but didn't? What could you have done?
- If a situation seems unsafe for you to intervene, what else might you do?

Video resources

Watch "The Story of Pink Shirt Day" and other videos on YouTube and the Pink Shirt Day website, *http://pinkshirtday.ca/*, and discuss how to support bystanders to stop bullying.

Women of Courage

Heroes inspire us. They move us to action when otherwise we might remain stagnant. Role models help us figure out how we want to live in the world. Heroes can be found everywhere, not only in the usual places like history and storybooks, but even in our own extended families and neighborhoods. When we look around, we find people who are standing up for what's right all around us.

This Torah portion is filled with heroes. The heroes in the beginning of the portion are mostly ordinary women who display extraordinary courage. Pharaoh, the evil Egyptian king, orders the midwives to kill every male child when they deliver Israelite babies. The midwives disobey Pharaoh. Pharaoh then orders every male Israelite baby to be thrown into the Nile. Moses's mother, Yocheved, hides Moses, and then his sister Miriam and the Pharaoh's daughter save his life. Pharaoh's daughter adopts Moses as her own son and raises him in the Egyptian palace.

The midwives, Yocheved, Miriam, and Pharaoh's daughter all have the strength to disobey an evil decree and sustain life. As far as we know, they were not encouraged to do what they did from an outside source. Rather they had a strong sense of right and wrong and acted from that internal compass. Figuring out who our role models are helps shape our own internal moral compasses.

—*by Rabbi Dianne Cohler-Esses*

> "Every boy that is born you shall throw into the Nile, but let every girl live."
>
> (Exodus 1:22)

MAKING CONNECTIONS

- Who are your heroes? Why do you look up to them?
- What have they done that inspires you?
- What would you like to do in your life to inspire others?

Role models/heroes poster

Make a group poster. Ask each person to contribute a picture of a hero or role model, or a saying or teaching from someone they admire.

When Should Patience Overcome Passion?

"Let My people go."
(Exodus 5:1)

Patience is a skill that we develop over time. Young children cannot wait patiently. Over the years, we learn to wait and to control our impulses and desires.

When Moses first sees the suffering of his brothers and sisters, he responds with a primal sense of justice. When he sees an Egyptian striking an Israelite, he kills the Egyptian and hides his body. There are clearly other ways Moses could have handled the situation. Apparently his ability to be patient had not evolved. Later Moses encounters God at the burning bush, and God bestows upon him a mission to save his people. Now Moses's individual sense of justice and murderous outrage is transformed into a sense of national mission. He goes to Pharaoh again and again, undeterred, repeating God's words "Let My people go," instead of lashing out aggressively.

We can all learn, like Moses, to transform our natural impulses into something higher. We can learn to use peaceful yet forceful words and to ask for what we want civilly, rather than hitting, lashing out, or throwing a childish tantrum. From the midst of our passions and impulses, we can learn to behave constructively and wisely, habits that will serve us well throughout our lives. Following the example of Moses and others who model restraint, we can internalize self-control.

—*by Rabbi Dianne Cohler-Esses*

MAKING CONNECTIONS

- What do you do when you get angry? How else could you respond?
- What are the best ways to deal with unfair situations?

Social action

Make a list of causes your group feels passionately about. Choose one and write personal letters to elected officials or others about the changes you want to see. Discuss other options for social action.

Accepting Responsibility

Most of us resist accepting responsibility at one time or another. Responsibilities can be challenging and feel burdensome. Sometimes we are inundated by activities, chores, and schoolwork and we can start to feel overwhelmed. It's important to find the right balance between work and play, between structured time and free time.

Perhaps we can learn something about accepting responsibility from this biblical portion. At the burning bush, Moses does not want to accept the responsibility of freeing his people from slavery. Moses is afraid that neither the Pharaoh nor his own people will listen to him. Moses is a stutterer and feels deeply insecure about his ability to communicate and stand up to Pharaoh.

In the end, Moses is able to accept responsibility. God, understanding that Moses is anxious about communicating, appoints Moses's brother Aaron as a spokesperson. God helps Moses compensate for his weakness. When we see that we have more than we can handle, we can reach out for help from others. We can talk about our weaknesses and insecurities and get help to compensate for them.

—by Rabbi Dianne Cohler-Esses

> "How then should Pharaoh heed me, a man of impeded speech!"
> (Exodus 6:12)

MAKING CONNECTIONS

- Which responsibilities are hardest for you?
- What do you think might help you meet these responsibilities?
- How can we balance our time in order to meet our responsibilities but not feel overwhelmed?

Levels of responsibility

Make four poster boards with the following titles: personal, family, community, global. Have group members list their responsible actions in each of these areas. Are there things we do that overlap? (For example, when taking out recycling, I am helping my family keep our home clean while fulfilling my global responsibility to our planet.) Should certain responsibilities take priority? Why?

VA'EIRA

"I will harden Pharaoh's heart."
(Exodus 7:3)

Free Will

Try telling a teacher, parent, or friend that you just *had* to do something they deem inappropriate. Nine times out of ten, the response will be "That's ridiculous! Nobody can force you to do something!" We have a deep belief in, and awareness of, our freedom to choose our own behavior.

In this Torah portion, *Va'eira*, God informs Moses that God will harden Pharaoh's heart, and Pharaoh will refuse to release the Jews from captivity. Pharaoh's heart is "artificially" hardened by God, but in normal life situations, humans are in fact free to choose between right and wrong.

Throughout life, we encounter decisions. As we grow, the nature of these challenges shift, but what remains constant is our ability to choose our own path. For teens, this may take the form of taking school seriously, resisting smoking, or being kind to others. For people facing serious hardships, all they may be able to choose is how to react with a positive attitude. There is always a choice to be made. We can turn every moment into a victory by making good choices. Let's celebrate the gift of choice!

—*by Rabbi Moshe Becker*

MAKING CONNECTIONS

- Have friends ever pressured you to do something you didn't want to do?
- Do you have clear limits? Things you won't do no matter what?
- What decisions are you most proud of that were hard to make?

Peer pressure scenarios

Make some index cards with scenarios in which friends try to pressure a friend to do something he or she doesn't want to do. Role-play these scenarios. Each scene should have one or more people pressuring a friend, in person or by text message. Others in the room can help the person being pressured by suggesting responses he or she might try. After the scenario is over, ask the person who was pressured to share how it felt to be in that situation.

Freedom with Limits

"Let My people go to worship Me."

(Exodus 9:1)

Have you ever tried to play Monopoly or another game without rules? Rules give a framework and structure to any game or sport and help make the game fun. Without the rules, the activity could not work. Similarly, rules give structure to our lives.

In this Torah portion, *Va'eira*, Moses demands that Pharaoh free the Israelites from slavery. Moses is clear why he wants the people's freedom: so that they may serve God. Moses is not seeking absolute freedom for the children of Israel. Rather, he is seeking to take them from Pharaoh's harsh rule to the loving guidance of God. Moses knows that unbridled freedom would not be beneficial to anyone. He knows that rules and structures will be liberating for the Israelites.

Though we may bristle at the idea of restrictions placed on us, we also see how we flourish when given clear, easily understood rules. Limits, instructions, and guidelines help us to accomplish tasks and fulfill our responsibilities. They enable us to find balance. From speed limits to job descriptions, we, like the children of Israel, can feel more free with such guidelines.

—*by Rabbi Judith Greenberg*

MAKING CONNECTIONS

- Who makes the rules you follow?
- What is a rule that you wish more people followed?
- What do you think makes something a good rule? A bad rule?

Game without rules

Try playing a board game for a few turns using no rules. See if and how it works. Discuss whether and why rules are necessary to make the game a success.

Bo

A Stubborn Heart

> "I will bring but one more plague . . . after that he shall let you go."
>
> (Exodus 11:1)

All of us can become stubborn at times and refuse to listen to what others are telling us about ourselves. It's hard to change, and we may resist listening to difficult truths.

So it is with Pharaoh, the leader of Egypt, in this Torah portion. He does not want to listen to Moses and let the Israelites go. He hardens his heart, and plague after plague ensues.

When we refuse to listen, life becomes harder. We become "plagued" with problems. But we can work to change our stubbornness. Gentleness is the key with ourselves and with others. The more we push, the more others push back, the more stubbornness we encounter. On the other hand, going softly often makes for less resistance.

—by Rabbi Dianne Cohler-Esses

MAKING CONNECTIONS

- Have you ever been in a situation where you wanted to make up with a friend, sibling, or parent but found it difficult to do so?
- What makes people become stubborn?
- What can help people be less stubborn?

Human sculpture

The opposite of stubborn is flexible. This game will help your brain and body to be more flexible. Break into small groups. Choose a leader, and have the leader pick a subject and try to shape the participants in that group into a human sculpture of that thing. But first the participants should stand still like statues and resist the leader's attempt to move or shape them. Then participants make their bodies and minds flexible, and they brainstorm to help the leader shape them into that human sculpture.

46

Family Stories from Generation to Generation

Certain stories get told in families over and over again, stories of how our family came to be who we are and do what we do, stories from our grandparents and great-grandparents, stories that often include immigration and making it in America, as well as how life used to be in the "olden" days. These family stories feed our imagination, giving us a sense of who we are in the world as well as resources to face our own daily struggles.

The story of our liberation from Egypt, told in this Torah portion, is our story of origin; it is the story of how we came to be who we are as a people. The Torah teaches that we must pass on this story to our children. At the Passover seder, we retell the story and remember that we were slaves in Egypt and were freed by God. We also recall the Exodus from Egypt in the Friday night Kiddush and in the daily recitation of the Sh'ma.

Storytelling is vital in any family. There are different genres of storytelling, all vital in their own way. There are fairytales and myths and stories about what children face as they grow up. There are family stories, and then there are the stories of our people, the foundational stories that form our collective identity and are transmitted from generation to generation. Stories about what the Israelites experienced as slaves in Egypt and how they were delivered from slavery can promote moral development and create a sense that we belong to something larger. These stories remind us that we are an ancient people who have survived to this day to tell the tale.

—*by Rabbi Dianne Cohler-Esses*

> "This day shall be to you one of remembrance: you shall celebrate it as a festival."
> (Exodus 12:14)

MAKING CONNECTIONS

- What are your favorite stories?
- What do you like best about one of your favorite stories?
- Why is it important that we continue to tell stories?

Family stories

Ask each participant to tell a favorite family story in three to five minutes. Give them lead time to prepare and plan their story. After the storytelling, discuss whether there were common themes or motifs in the stories.

Do Not Be Locked in the Past

> "Tell the people to borrow . . . objects of silver and gold."
>
> (Exodus 11:2)

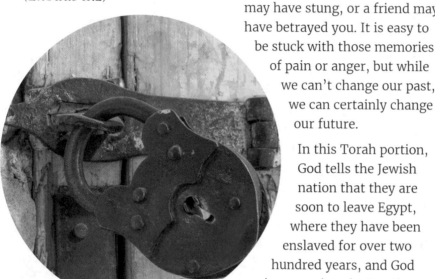

There is a huge difference between living with the past and living in the past. You may have been cheated by someone. A teacher's words may have stung, or a friend may have betrayed you. It is easy to be stuck with those memories of pain or anger, but while we can't change our past, we can certainly change our future.

In this Torah portion, God tells the Jewish nation that they are soon to leave Egypt, where they have been enslaved for over two hundred years, and God gives a curious instruction. The soon-to-be-free slaves are to approach their Egyptian neighbors—their masters—who will gladly give them gifts of value. This is not compensation for the years of misery the Jewish nation endured. Gifts cannot erase the memories of slavery, but they may take the sting off. Knowing your past is of value; being caught in your past has no value. The future is bright as long as you are willing to focus forward, not backward.

Have you ever heard the phrase "so-and-so lives in the past"? This is what happens when a person cannot let go of his or her experiences and is unable to move forward. We must remember the past and learn from it without constantly reliving emotions and experiences. Truly great people are those who can retain their memories, learn from them, and focus on creating a bright future.

—by Rabbi Moshe Becker

MAKING CONNECTIONS

- Why do you think people hold on to feelings of anger or hate?
- Can you give an example of a time that you held on to a grudge or remained angry for a long time?
- What helped you let go of those feelings?

Dissolving anger

Get some spy paper (can be purchased online or in specialty stores). Think of something from the past you are angry about and write it on the paper. Put the spy paper in water and watch your anger and resentments disappear!

The Faith to Go Forward

It has been said that 90 percent of life is showing up. Being willing to get involved, to show up, to make the phone call, to introduce yourself, can bring outsized results. Taking the initiative can give you momentum to bring you closer to your goals.

In this *parashah*, the Israelites leave Egypt and are cornered at the sea by the Egyptians. The Israelites are terrified and about to give up hope. The only one who has the courage to walk into the sea and follow Moses's instructions is Nachshon. As told in the Midrash, Nachshon walks in past his ankles, past his knees, past his waist, and keeps on going even though it doesn't seem that the water will ever recede. The Red Sea opens up only when Nachshon is up to his neck, and because of him the children of Israel are able to pass through on dry land.

There are times when life is really difficult. Issues can hit us from all sides. Whether they are financial, academic, or social problems or even those of a more serious nature like disability, illness, or loss, it can feel as if we are drowning in a sea of difficulties. But the way forward can be as simple as just keeping going even though it may feel that we are walking straight into impossibility. We must maintain faith that something will open up, so that we can keep on going until a path becomes visible.

—*by Rabbi Dianne Cohler-Esses*

> "Moses held out his arm. . . . The waters were split."
> (Exodus 14:21)

MAKING CONNECTIONS

- Do you ever agree to go first for a school activity or other challenge? Is it scary? What makes it so?
- Do you think you could be a "Nachshon"? Why or why not?

Living examples

Ask each participant to bring in a story of a living "Nachshon," someone who has put himself or herself out there to make change. Discuss their stories and what we can learn from them.

What's the Use of Complaining?

"The people grumbled against Moses."
(Exodus 15:24)

"This is boring!" "When are we going to get there?" "He has more toys than I do!" Have you ever heard these complaints or made them yourself? It can be easy to feel frustrated or deprived.

In this Torah portion, the children of Israel also complain. After passing through the Red Sea and arriving safely in the wilderness, the first thing they do is whine. "We don't have any food or water!" "We're going to die in the desert!" Though they are granted sweet water to drink and manna falls down from the sky, they continue to complain throughout their time in the wilderness. Their life in Egypt was a period of terrible hardship and enslavement, yet once in the wilderness, they recall it as a time when they had everything they needed.

How can we feel gratitude for the blessings in our lives, rather than focusing on what we don't have or what is difficult? When there is an impulse to complain, it helps to shift our mind-set to a sense of gratitude for all the good in our lives. Doing something as prosaic as keeping a gratitude journal or list makes us more attuned to what we do have than to what is missing or in short supply. Even if hardship or illness has visited us or those we love, we can still be grateful for the many blessings we have. Stressing the positive aspects of our lives, rather than reinforcing negatives, can be powerful.

—*by Rabbi Dianne Cohler-Esses*

MAKING CONNECTIONS

- For what things in your life are you grateful?
- What do you wish was different in your life and why?
- Does complaining get results or just release tension?
- Do you admire people in ill health or in difficult situations who rarely complain?

Gratitude journal

Provide each participant with a small, blank book. Make a project of decorating and personalizing the covers. This is a personal gratitude journal for writing what you are grateful for. Experiment with writing at least three lines every night for two weeks. Then discuss how it felt and what you learned.

Humility

"For who are we that you should grumble against us?"
(Exodus 16:7)

What gives us our sense of our own value and worth? Is it our accomplishments or recognition from others? Is it possible to be humble and self-confident at the same time?

We can learn an important message from Moses. In this portion, his authority is challenged by disgruntled members of the Jewish nation. Moses is well aware of his special relationship with God and the responsibility he carries as leader. Nonetheless, he truly does not view those achievements as reason for arrogance. Moses is a confident leader but a humble man, recognizing that everything he has is a gift and not an entitlement.

We all need to find balance. We have innate talents and successes we've attained through hard work, but we can still be humble. Humility is living with the understanding that we are simply doing our part by making a unique contribution to the world using the tools and strengths that God has given us. We all have those unique capabilities, so let's respect ourselves and each other while remaining humble.

—by Rabbi Moshe Becker

MAKING CONNECTIONS

- What are you good at, either naturally or through hard work?
- What does recognition mean to you? Why is it important or unimportant?
- Can you laugh at yourself?
- Can making yourself small help you feel big inside?

Appreciating others

Read the story "Who Packed Your Parachute?" (this short vignette can be found online in several versions). Make a list of people who help you during the day (parents, street cleaners, custodial staff, teachers, supermarket checkers, and so on). Make a thank-you card for someone who "packs your parachute."

YITRO

Finding the Correct Balance

> "Israel encamped there in front of the mountain [Sinai]."
>
> (Exodus 19:2)

People will take greater notice of our actions than our boasting about them. One of the most important things we can learn is to think of others. Being sensitive to the feelings of others and having a humble spirit come naturally to some, but most need guidance to develop these skills.

In this Torah portion, God reveals the Ten Commandments and Torah at Mount Sinai, a small, low, nondescript mountain. Rabbinic legend (Midrash) explains why God did not choose other bigger, more beautiful, and grander mountains that all promoted themselves and expected to be chosen. God deliberately chose the unimpressive Mount Sinai to show us the value of humility.

Humility in no way means low self-esteem. According to Rav Kook, the first chief rabbi of Israel, we should conduct ourselves with humility but at the same time consider ourselves to be of high worth because of our good qualities. The ancient rabbis were much more concerned with our being overconfident and arrogant than our being too accommodating to others. An excellent test of being humble in spirit is the way we treat others of lesser abilities than ourselves. Do we treat them as inferior, or are we able to admire others for the strengths they have?

—by Rabbi Dianne Cohler-Esses

MAKING CONNECTIONS

- When you are feeling self-confidence and pride in your achievements, how do you maintain humility?
- Is there a downside to being too humble?
- Does humility make us more or less accepting of the little annoyances of life?

Two notes

Rabbi Simcha Bunam Bonhart of Przysucha (1765–1827) used to say, "Everyone must have two pockets, with a note in each pocket. . . . When feeling lowly and depressed, discouraged or disconsolate, one should reach into the right pocket and find there the words 'For my sake was the world created.' But when feeling high and mighty, one should reach into the left pocket and find the words 'I am but dust and ashes'" (from Martin Buber, *Tales of the Hasidim, Later Masters* [New York: Schocken Books,1978], pp. 249–50). Make these two notes and put them in your pockets. Walk around with them for a few days and then share about your experience.

Learning from Everyone

Intelligence may be in our genes, but wisdom is certainly not. We become wise when we realize that everything in our lives is an opportunity to learn something. Everything that happens to us and everyone we know (yes, everyone) can teach us something. The rabbis expressed this in the Ethics of the Fathers (*Pirkei Avot*) 4:1 saying, "Who is wise? One who learns from every person."

In this Torah portion, Moses listens carefully to the suggestions of Jethro (in Hebrew, Yitro), his father-in-law, and implements them. Moses is the greatest of all prophets. He communicates directly with God and receives the Torah. Yet Moses has the humility and the wisdom to heed Jethro's advice on how to reorganize the courts most efficiently, by appointing a middle level of judges.

No matter how accomplished we are, there is always more to learn. The lessons often come in unexpected and surprising ways when we are willing to see life as a learning experience. The people we learn from need not be our superiors. Each and every person we interact with can teach us something. If we are open to learning the "unconventional" lessons of life, we become wise and inspire those around us to wisdom as well. Let's turn intelligence into wisdom!

—by Rabbi Moshe Becker

> "You shall also seek out from among all the people capable men who fear God."
> (Exodus 18:21)

MAKING CONNECTIONS

- Name something positive you have learned from a friend.
- Name something you have learned from a sibling.
- Have you ever learned something important when you were not expecting to? Why was it unexpected?

Learning styles

There are several quizzes available online to find out about your own learning style. Take the quiz and discuss the way your learning style affects how you learn from others.

YITRO

Listening or Really Hearing

"The thing you are doing is not right; you will surely wear yourself out."
(Exodus 18:17-18)

Picture the following exchange: Sarah shares a story that is important to her with her friend Adam. He seems distracted, and she asks if he is paying attention. He assures her that he is indeed listening. But Sarah retorts, "Okay, you are listening, but did you hear me?" Everyone can imagine a conversation like this. The distinction between being listened to and being heard is crucial to the way Sarah feels in this situation. She doesn't just want someone to listen to her words, she wants to be "heard" or understood.

In this Torah portion, Jethro, Moses's father-in-law, observes Moses at work and offers him what we might call "constructive criticism." Moses, like all of us, is human, and there are a number of ways that he might receive this feedback. However, instead of getting defensive or passing it off as irrelevant, Moses takes the opportunity to truly hear Jethro's words, and he changes his course of action based on his new understanding of the situation.

It can often be difficult to truly hear what others are saying to us, especially when we are presented with new ideas or criticism. Being able to go beyond listening requires an open ear, an open mind, and an open heart. When we listen more deeply, we engage the speaker in a more meaningful way, and we allow ourselves to be affected by their words. This comes from an intentional shift in the way we approach the conversation. It is easy to simply "listen" to someone. We stand to benefit much more deeply if we open ourselves up to truly hear them.

—by Rabbi Kerrith Rosenbaum

MAKING CONNECTIONS

- When was a time you think you were not truly heard? How did that feel?
- Was there ever a time when you listened to someone and they did not feel heard? What could you have changed about that interaction?
- How can you work to keep an open mind when you are hearing new or difficult things?

Retelling stories

Work in pairs. One person reads or tells a story, and the other person has to repeat it back. You can also do this with pictures. One person reads a story while the other person draws the story in a picture. Talk about what you learned about listening and hearing from this exercise.

Fun versus Principles

Often in life we look for the fireworks, the fun ride, the sparkling party, but it's the everyday, the prosaic, that actually creates the infrastructure for a solid life.

Consider what happens in this Torah portion. After the thunder, voices, and lightning at Sinai in the last *parashah*, in this portion we find law after law. Such a letdown after the terrifying excitement of Sinai! But what we find here are really the tenets of how to live life and how to live with one another on a daily basis. Some examples: "You must not carry false rumors" (Exodus 23:1); "You shall not oppress a stranger" (Exodus 23:9); "On the seventh day you shall cease from labor" (Exodus 23:12). Each principle provides instructions for daily living.

We may focus more on fun times than on principles, but the guidelines and boundaries embedded in our day-to-day behavior are even more important than fun times. We need to be sure to focus on how we treat people, both inside and outside our families, and how we manage our day-to-day lives.

—by Rabbi Dianne Cohler-Esses

"These are the rules that you shall set."
(Exodus 21:1)

....

MAKING CONNECTIONS

- How do we treat the people who serve our needs, such as waiters, bus drivers, cashiers, or household helpers?
- What helps us figure out how to treat others?
- Which values are most important to you? How do you express these values?

Family rules

Work in small groups and make a list of rules for your ideal family. What rules or guidelines would you have to ensure that family members treat each other well?

Insults Leave a Lasting Impact

> **"You must not carry false rumors."**
> (Exodus 23:1)

We must carefully value our speech. Words are a powerful tool. They can bring people closer or they can distance them. They can hurt or they can heal. Whether we are speaking to a family member, a friend, a teacher, a neighbor, or a stranger, our words always have an impact. Our tone and manner of speaking affect the person to whom we are speaking. If we are insulting or disrespectful, we become a problem to others and to ourselves.

This Torah portion emphasizes that the words we speak to others have definite consequences. The Torah is teaching us to be very careful and to measure our words, for insults are easy to give but hard to retract. This topic is so important to Judaism that our daily prayers always emphasize the importance of proper speech.

Learning to speak in a thoughtful and considerate way takes repeated practice throughout life. When we are tired, upset, or distracted, a quick insulting remark or response may arise. Therefore, we all need tools to remind us to speak kindly and thoughtfully so that we can learn to avoid verbal damage.

—*by Rabbi Moshe Becker*

MAKING CONNECTIONS

- In what way can speech be used positively or negatively?
- How should one speak if angry or feeling attacked?
- What's the best way to react if you're insulted by someone?

Compliments tag

Give each person a pen and a pad of sticky notes. Write a list of positive qualities on the board, exactly the same number as you have participants. When you say ready, set, go, players have to write each word on the notepad and stick it to a different person to whom it applies; each person must place one tag on each other person. The first person to compliment all the other players wins. You can do a quieter version of this by having each person stand in the middle of a circle and other people give sincere compliments. Talk about how it feels to give and receive compliments.

Keep Your Distance from Lying

> "Keep far from a false charge."
>
> (Exodus 23:7)

We all know the story of America's first president, George Washington, who chopped down the cherry tree. When confronted with his behavior, he stated, "I cannot tell a lie." Though it is honorable that Washington chose to tell the truth, he could have avoided lying in a different way. He could have considered his actions from the outset and avoided chopping down the tree.

Torah portion *Mishpatim* warns us to avoid falsehood. The wording is unlike any other instruction or warning in the Torah. Instead of simply saying, "Don't lie," the Torah states, "Keep far" from falsehood. The Torah is encouraging us to be mindful of our actions and their potential consequences. We can stay far away from lying and deception by avoiding actions we may be tempted to lie about. If we cannot tell the truth about something or feel the need to hide it, it is probably not a good idea to do it.

Suppose you are approached by a classmate who asks you to help him or her cheat on an upcoming test. It may be difficult to resist cheating However, if you are caught, you will have to choose between admitting to a misdeed and lying. We can "keep far" from the temptation to lie by considering the results of our decisions before we make them.

—by Rabbi Moshe Becker

MAKING CONNECTIONS

- Why is lying wrong?
- If you knew you would have to tell someone about what you did, do you think it would stop you from doing something bad?
- Do you trust people who you know tell lies?
- Is it okay to deceive someone if you don't technically tell a lie? Why or why not?

Truth in your heart

Psalm 15 states that the one who can dwell in the house of God is one who "speaks the truth in his heart." In contrast, studies show that pathological liars often believe they are telling the truth. Write down some truths from your heart in your journal. What does it mean to tell yourself the truth?

T'RUMAH

There's No Place Like Home

> "Let them make Me a sanctuary that I may dwell among them."
> (Exodus 25:8)

The old adage says there's no place like home. At the end of a tiring day or a vacation, it's so comforting to come home and snuggle up in one's very own bed.

This *parashah* is about building a sanctuary, a home for God. A sanctuary is a holy place where God will meet with human beings. God's sanctuary is a beautiful place, made with precious materials of gold, stones, and wood. There is a certain place within this beautiful home, between two cherubim, that God says will be a meeting point between the divine and the human.

As we design our own homes, it is important to think about how our meeting places are organized. Are they organized around a computer or a television, or are they set up so that family members will have eye contact and conversation? An interesting exercise is to scan our home in our mind's eye to note how many places are focused around isolated activities and how many around being together with family and/or visitors.

—by Rabbi Dianne Cohler-Esses

MAKING CONNECTIONS

- What do you like best about being home?
- What is your favorite part of your home?
- What is your least favorite part of your home?

Collage

Take photos of places in your home or outdoors that feel to you like sanctuaries. Make a collage of the photos. This can also be done with pictures printed from online or cut from magazines. Discuss what makes these places feel like sanctuaries.

58

What Is Inside Us Is Most Important

"Overlay it with pure gold—overlay it inside and out."
(Exodus 25:11)

As we grow, we are trying to develop ourselves. We spend time improving our appearance, learning the styles we like, and choosing how we wear our hair. Often we spend more time on our exterior than on our interior.

This Torah portion describes building the sanctuary in the desert. Instructions are clear that the outside should be plain, orderly, and neat, but not showy. The inside is clearly more important than the outside and holds the most beautiful decorations and objects. Our bodies are our own sanctuary. Clearly, in Judaism how we develop our inside, the inner us, is most important.

Of course, it is important for people to feel good about how they look on the outside. The Torah's message is that you should look good on the outside but never forget to focus on your inner development. We can all work on developing our inner qualities. Just as we turn to others for advice about how to dress or what looks best, we can also learn from them about the positive inner qualities we seek to develop.

—by Fred Claar

MAKING CONNECTIONS

- What are the best qualities inside you?
- What other qualities would you like to possess inside?
- How could you develop other good qualities inside?

Who am I?

For this activity, you will need a roll of brown paper and markers. Have each person lie on the paper while others outline his or her body with markers. Give each person the full-size outline to fill in. Participants use markers, pictures, and words to fill in the outline with the inner qualities to which they aspire.

T'RUMAH

Chores and "a Willing Heart"

"You shall accept gifts for Me from everyone whose heart so moves them."

(Exodus 25:2)

We may complain about doing chores. Often we do these things unwillingly, grudgingly. We need to be coaxed, chided, and threatened before fulfilling our responsibilities. It can take a lot of moaning and groaning for us to be responsible.

In this Torah portion, the Israelites offer materials and skills to build the sanctuary. However, not everyone has to give, only "everyone whose heart is willing." The people of Israel ultimately give freely and generously with an open heart, each contributing what they can in order to build the sacred sanctuary. In the end, there is more than enough.

In an ideal world, we would fulfill our responsibilities with a "willing heart" instead of whining and complaining through our chores. No one can really force someone else to have a better attitude. We have to choose our own attitude toward our responsibilities. We can look on them as burdens or as our way of contributing to the common goal of a comfortable home and happy life.

—by Rabbi Dianne Cohler-Esses

MAKING CONNECTIONS

- Which chores are hardest for you? Why?
- Why are chores and obligations important to do?
- Resisting chores may be a habit. What steps can help us develop a better attitude toward chores?

Fifteen-minute cleanup

Agree to a fifteen-minute cleanup of home, school, or classroom. Two people should be in charge of choosing upbeat music for the cleanup. Have all supplies ready and tasks assigned beforehand. When the music starts, everyone has to move as fast as possible to complete the cleanup. After fifteen minutes, stop the music. How do you feel? Do you want to keep going? What have you learned about chores and a "willing heart"?

The Meaning of Clothes

Since the Garden of Eden, people have often been self-conscious about their bodies and exhibited a desire for privacy. We cover up our bodies with clothing of infinite variety. Styles—sophisticated, slinky, funky, professional, or fun—send a very personal message to the world. Clothing reflects how we value ourselves and our bodies.

In this *parashah*, the priests who serve in the sanctuary dress for "dignity and adornment." Both those reasons are crucial. The dignity of the priests' role is reflected in the elaborate clothes they wear, complete with sashes, breastplate, and headdress. But the priests' clothes are not only about dignity; they are also very beautiful. They are made in bright colors—clear blue, purple, and crimson—with golden bells and pomegranates, made out of linen and embroidered work.

Reflect on the various ways you dress when you play different roles in the world. How do your clothes communicate the values of beauty and dignity?

—*by Rabbi Dianne Cohler-Esses*

"Make sacral vestments for your brother Aaron, for dignity and adornment."
(Exodus 28:2)

MAKING CONNECTIONS

- Which are your favorite clothes? Why?
- What do your clothes say about you?
- How do you feel about getting dressed up to go to a special event? Is it important to get dressed up for special events? Why?

Clothing drive

Find an organization in your area that collects clothes, and organize a clothing drive for your school or community. You can collect all kinds of items or focus on something specific like new underwear and socks or coats, hats, and gloves for winter.

T'TZAVEH

Let Everyone Shine

"You shall bring forward your brother Aaron, with his sons."
(Exodus 28:1)

We all have talents and abilities, as do our siblings and friends. At times we have difficulty recognizing a sister's talents; at other times we may be jealous of a brother's unique capabilities. We must develop the confidence in ourselves to the point that we can let our brothers and sisters shine.

This Torah portion teaches us about the appointment of Aaron and of his descendants as high priests forever. This is a permanent and important role that is granted to Aaron and his family. Moses, who spent his life fighting for the freedom of the Jewish nation, does not receive this honor. The descendants of Moses receive no particular place in the future of the Israelite people. Yet Moses readily and happily steps aside to allow Aaron to come forth and shine in his priestly glory.

Families are made up of individuals who together form a unit. Just as our body has different limbs for different functions but is still one body, so a family has different members with different strengths. Allowing each individual's particular talents to find expression strengthens the entire unit. By acknowledging and celebrating a sibling's personality, we not only affirm his or her importance as an individual but strengthen ourselves as well. Everyone deserves a chance to shine!

—*by Rabbi Moshe Becker*

....

MAKING CONNECTIONS

- What are some unique strengths your siblings or friends have?
- What is a unique strength you have?
- Is it hard to think of or acknowledge the strengths of others?
- What can you do to help affirm others' talents?

Talent show

You can make this as large or small as you want. People who don't want to perform can be involved in directing, arranging the order of the acts, setting up scenes, lighting, making programs, publicity, and ushering. Find a role for each person in making the talent show happen.

Tension between Silence and Sound

Most of us are familiar with the biblical saying "To everything there is a season." In the Book of Ecclesiastes, this adage is followed with examples such as a "a time to weep and a time to laugh; a time to mourn and a time to dance . . . a time to keep silent and a time to speak" (Ecclesiastes 3:1, 4, 7). When is the time to keep silent and when should we speak?

In this Torah portion, *T'tzaveh*, we see an example of the tension between silence and sound. The text includes descriptions of the priestly garments, the clothes Aaron and his sons wear for their priestly duties. The garments have both little bells and yarn tassels. When the priests move, the bells make noise but the tassels do not. On this holy piece of clothing, both are present.

It is important to speak up and share our voices. It is good to share our opinions and ideas, to share positive feedback, to say hello, and to ask meaningful questions. We have the potential to make others feel good about themselves when we speak up. But our voices can also be hurtful. We should be careful not to use our voices to spread gossip or lies, and we should be careful with our words. Perhaps the moments in which we should remain silent are the times when our words could cause harm. To everything there is a season, a time to keep silent and a time to speak.

—*by Rabbi Kerrith Rosenbaum*

> "A golden bell and a pomegranate [of yarn], all around the hem of the robe."
>
> (Exodus 28:34)

MAKING CONNECTIONS

- When was a time you spoke out? Was it the right moment to speak out?
- Is there a time when you spoke but perhaps should not have?
- Is there a time when you kept silent but should not have?
- Are you aware of your body language and facial expressions when you are silent? Do they sometimes speak for you?

Silent meditation

Practice ten to fifteen minutes of silent meditation together. You can begin with a guided meditation text or some simple instructions. Afterward, go around in a circle sharing about your experience of the silence.

Ki Tisa

Waiting: Patience Is a Companion of Wisdom

"When the people saw that Moses was so long in coming down from the mountain . . ."

(Exodus 32:1)

Waiting is difficult. When we are waiting, for instance, for a friend to call, the time can feel excruciatingly long. Patience hopefully comes with age, but even then it is a hard-earned attribute.

In this Torah portion, the children of Israel wait forty days and forty nights for Moses to come down the mountain with the Torah. They are worried that Moses will never return to them and frightened that they will have no leader to bring them to the Promised Land. They are so scared that they build themselves an idol, a Golden Calf, to accompany them through the desert. Descending from Mount Sinai, Moses witnesses his people worshipping the Golden Calf. He becomes so angry that he hurls the Ten Commandments he just received to the ground, and the stone tablets shatter into fragments.

Being able to wait requires developing self-control. Patience is an acquired skill. How can we learn to have patience? It can be done little by little. The next time you are stuck waiting in line or for a bus, remind yourself that you are building your patience skills.

—by Rabbi Dianne Cohler-Esses

MAKING CONNECTIONS

- When is it hardest to wait?
- When do you become frustrated?
- What helps you when you are waiting?
- Why is patience important?

Old-fashioned potato relay race

You need a potato for each person and a large spoon and bucket for each team. This should be done in a large outdoor space or hall. Make teams of three to six players. Line buckets up facing each team a distance from where they stand (usually about fifteen to thirty feet away). Each participant must carry a potato on a spoon and drop it in the bucket, then run back so the next player can go. If the potato drops, the player must start from the beginning. Talk about how this game requires patience (not dropping the potato, waiting for team members). How did it feel to play?

Rejuvenate Yourself Weekly

Our lives are full of commitments, responsibilities, school, and work. Often we are caught up in the demands of our lives and easily forget to focus on what is most important to us: our families and our "inner selves." When the pressures of daily life take over without giving us a break, difficulties eventually strike.

Thousands of years ago, before the Torah, time was broken only into months by the moon. The Torah introduced the concept of weeks for the first time in history. Not only did the Torah break time into weeks, it also created, for the first time, the concept of a day of rest each week, Shabbat. Shabbat sanctifies time and is the antidote to our busy, pressure-filled lives, presenting us with healthy limits. Shabbat allows us time to express gratitude for our blessings, time to relax and enjoy our family and community.

Celebrating Shabbat is not always easy. It is a worthwhile challenge to cut back a busy pressure-filled life, but it cannot be accomplished overnight. Think about celebrating Shabbat as learning a musical instrument. Nobody goes from a beginner to expert immediately. Start with small doable steps, such as observing part of the day at first. On Shabbat do things that are different from other days, making your rest special. Your body, soul, and family require rejuvenation. Give them all a break.

—by Fred Claar

"It [the Shabbat] shall be a sign for all time between Me and the people of Israel."
(Exodus 31:17)

MAKING CONNECTIONS

- Do you think a day of rest each week is a good idea?
- How could you begin to bring sacred time each week into your life?
- How would you spend your special sacred time weekly?

Decorate a phone bag

Many people choose to unplug from their devices on Shabbat. The National Day of Unplugging sells fabric bags to place phones in for the day of rest. Use these or another plain fabric bag. Decorate it with fabric markers or paint. Practice unplugging for Friday night or for all of Shabbat. How does it feel?

Ki Tisa

Cherishing What Is Broken

"[Moses] became enraged, and he hurled the tablets . . . and shattered them."
(Exodus 32:19)

We can be our own harshest critics. It is very easy to see our own flaws and what we could do better. We dwell on things in ourselves that others don't even notice. We may also see flaws in those around us and focus on those. But these flaws, like veins in a beautiful gem, are what remind us that we are each unique creations. Imagine how boring the world would be if we were all perfect.

Furious because the children of Israel built the Golden Calf in his absence, Moses throws the stone tablets containing the Ten Commandments to the ground nearly immediately after receiving them. They shatter into pieces. What happens to the shattered tablets? The obvious thing to do is to throw them away. But they are swept up and collected. They are kept and cherished alongside the new tablets that God commanded Moses to make.

The broken pieces of tablets are a metaphor for the parts of ourselves that are less than perfect. In the *parashah*, when the tablets were broken, we picked them up and valued the pieces. So too, we ought to cherish our broken pieces, the pieces that we might wish weren't there. These parts are sacred, and we need to "pick them up," with honor, in our life's journey.

—*by Rabbi Judith Greenberg*

MAKING CONNECTIONS

- Have you ever kept a toy even though it was broken? Why?
- What is one thing about yourself that you could try to like more?
- How can we learn to be more patient with ourselves and each other?

Recycled sculpture

You will need a hot glue gun, tape, staplers, and other art materials. Ask each person to bring at least one broken object from home. Spend time taking them apart and finding how you can make art from them. Display your sculptures together.

The Value of Rest

Families lead busy lives filled with work, homework, sports, lessons, running a household, and other activities. Often it seems there isn't a moment to breathe, a moment to just stop and say, "I'm here," and that's enough.

In this Torah portion, Moses tells the people that they are commanded to set aside the seventh day as a day of complete rest. It is a day in which no productive labor is allowed, a day in which the emphasis is put on "being" instead of "becoming" or "having."

Think about your own life. Is there enough time and room for simply stopping and being with one another? Stop now and take a breath. See how that feels. Think about ways to incorporate rest into the busy life of your family. Some families choose to put aside a day of the week and celebrate the Sabbath as a day of rest. Others pay attention to the principle of the day and figure out where to find the resting moments in life.

—*by Rabbi Dianne Cohler-Esses*

> "Six days work may be done, but on the seventh day you shall have a Sabbath of complete rest."
> (Exodus 35:2)

MAKING CONNECTIONS

- Do you find time to rest and relax?
- What does it mean to you to rest? Does it mean spending time with family or friends? Does it mean playing a game or reading a book?
- Which activities best put you at ease after a day or week of busyness?

Walking meditation

Walking meditation involves moving your body while quieting your mind. It teaches us to find restfulness even during movement. You can find a podcast with instructions for walking meditation by Rabbi Sheila Weinberg online at the Awakened Heart Project, or invite a meditation teacher to guide you in a walking meditation. After the meditation is over, talk about your experience. Did you find it restful or relaxing?

VAYAKHEIL

A Sacred Moment in Time

"You shall kindle no fire throughout your settlements on the Sabbath day."
(Exodus 35:3)

Are there special moments that you set aside to avoid interruptions or distractions, such as by choosing not to take phone calls or answer messages? Perhaps your family dinnertime, the fifteen minutes before bedtime, or a birthday celebration are such times for you. What is it that makes those times special? Is it the people you are with or what you are doing? Is it about a particular time of day or year or about the event itself? Now think about how those times feel different from the regular times. Are there certain things you choose to talk about or not talk about? How do you go about making that time special?

This Torah portion, *Vayakheil*, describes the sacred time of Shabbat in similar terms. At first glance it might seem that Shabbat is defined by a long list of things to "not do," but on closer look we can find that it is actually sharing a way of behaving that helps us to make that time—Shabbat—different and special.

For six days of the week we are limited in our actions because we are pulled in so many directions. We have great power to accomplish many things, but we are also constrained by our many responsibilities. One day, one special time, can help us to balance those responsibilities and limitations. Instead of thinking of Shabbat as being a time when there are lots of rules of things we "don't do," we can think of Shabbat as a time when we are free and have the power to create sacred moments in our lives.

—*by Rabbi Kerrith Rosenbaum*

MAKING CONNECTIONS

- What is a "sacred time" in your life?
- What do you do, or not do, in order to make time special?
- What are the things you might do, or not do, on Shabbat in order to make it more special for you?

Shabbat gathering

Plan a Shabbat gathering together. What will you do to make sacred time at your gathering? Whom will you invite? What "don't do" rules will you have? What will you do to make the time together special? You may wish to plan a special meal, special treats, songs, or activities.

Giving Is Justice in Action

VAYAKHEIL

Tzedakah, the Hebrew word for charity, actually translates as "justice." Giving charity is for everyone. Whether one has a lot or a little, giving is an integral part of a Jewish life. Even the poor are required to give charity. Money, food, our time, outgrown clothes, older toys, all can be useful to others in need. A community is only as strong as the willingness of its members to help each other.

This Torah portion, *Vayakheil*, stresses that every member of the community must participate in contributing to the building of the Mishkan, or Tabernacle. All are called upon to be "generous of spirit" (Exodus 35:5) and donate to the Tabernacle construction. All can be generous of spirit even with a small contribution.

We should think of our money, time, and possessions as tools we can use to benefit others. When we are willing to stand up and be counted for a charitable cause or for helping individuals in need, we become "generous of spirit" and display gratitude for what we have.

—*by Rabbi Moshe Becker*

"All men and women whose hearts moved them to bring anything . . ."
(Exodus 35:29)

MAKING CONNECTIONS

- Why is charity important?
- How does the giver benefit from giving charity?
- How can small amounts make a big difference? (Think of a savings account after many years.)
- Is it necessary to be recognized by others when giving?

Guest speaker

Invite a guest to speak to you, someone who is known for philanthropy or someone who has run a successful crowdfunding campaign. Find out more about how and why the speaker gives.

P'KUDEI

Does Our Behavior Match Our Priorities?

"A half-shekel
a head . . ."
(Exodus 38:26)

Most adults, especially those who have children, worry about money fairly often. We offset this worry by being accountable and conscious of the way we choose to spend our money. What we spend our money on reflects our priorities, and it is important that our behavior matches our priorities. Otherwise, there might be too little in the bank when it's time to pay for college!

In *Parashat P'kudei*, each person in the community is required to pay a half-shekel, reflecting the high priority placed on community by the Israelites. Moreover, accountability is evident in the detailed description of the way that half-shekel is to be used in the sanctuary.

It is a difficult challenge to have accountability in the context of our materialistic, consumption-focused society. Learning to save for the future is one important part of financial accountability. Another important part is setting priorities and not spending money we do not have. Making sure our financial behavior matches our priorities is key to success in our families and communities.

—*by Rabbi Dianne Cohler-Esses*

MAKING CONNECTIONS

- How do you feel when you spend money?
- Are you conscious of the value of money in meeting your priorities?
- What are other ways to realize your priorities without spending money?

Financial literacy

Financial literacy is not necessarily taught in school. You can graduate high school without ever learning how to make a household budget, how to save for a big purchase, or how to plan for retirement. Finance in the Classroom and Edutopia have links to in-person and online activities to build financial literacy. Choose an activity for your class, youth group, or family.

The Power of We

A great deal of work goes into running a household. Nothing happens by itself; someone must do the dishes, make lunches, drive carpool, go shopping, and so on. A lot of effort is involved, and everyone can pitch in.

In this Torah portion, the Jewish people complete the construction of the Tabernacle (Mishkan). All members of the community are required to do their part, commensurate with their abilities. Whether the contribution takes the form of a donation or volunteering, each and every person's involvement is a crucial element in reaching the final product. Only with everyone's participation does the Tabernacle become a sacred place.

It's easy to take our homes and synagogues for granted. Yet, it takes hard work to create and maintain them. A household can only function properly with the labors of hard-working family members, and a special environment can only be achieved by planning and effort. Everyone's contribution, and occasionally sacrifice, is necessary. Being a part of a family means thinking beyond our own needs. When all contribute according to their abilities, it makes a home a warm and welcoming place.

—*by Rabbi Moshe Becker*

"And when Moses saw that they had performed all the tasks . . . Moses blessed them."
(Exodus 39:43)

MAKING CONNECTIONS

- Name five actions or activities your parents do for your family.
- What do you do to pitch in? What more could you do?
- How do you feel when you know that others appreciate what you do?

Challah baking

Work together to make dough for challah baking. Make one challah or two small *challot* for each family. If it is early in the week, make dough that can be frozen and baked at home on Thursday or Friday.

LEVITICUS
VAYIKRA וַיִּקְרָא

Torah Topics

VAYIKRA

Rituals: Anchors for Our Lives

> "When any of you presents an offering of cattle to Adonai . . . he shall bring it to the Tent of Meeting."
>
> (Leviticus 1:2–3)

We all live with rituals. Whether it's the time and place we brush our teeth in the morning or the way we prepare for an assignment, rituals provide the infrastructure by which we live our lives. Without rituals, without certain consistent repetitions of behavior, our lives would be quite chaotic.

This Torah portion begins the third book of the Bible, Leviticus, and is full of details about ritual, especially those related to how and when to bring sacrifices. While prayer long ago replaced sacrifice in Jewish tradition, sacrifices were the original form of worship. Sacrifices were brought on many occasions for example: when one was guilty of sin, whether intentional or unintentional; when one was grateful; or when one was celebrating. The sacrificial system described in Leviticus provided a concrete way for people to express a wide range of emotions.

Sometimes, rituals may be performed by rote, as if they do not have significance. They can also be opportunities to signify something deeper, a learning or teaching moment, a chance to reflect and calm ourselves in the midst of our busy lives.

—*by Rabbi Dianne Cohler-Esses*

MAKING CONNECTIONS

- How do rituals enhance your feeling of well-being?
- What is your favorite family ritual?
- For what occasions would you like new rituals?
- Do you have rituals to express gratitude?

Circle of gratitude

Sit in a circle. Find an object that can be passed from person to person. The person who holds the object says something for which he or she is grateful. End the circle with a few minutes of silence or a song.

Rituals: Opportunities for Self-Improvement

Life is a beautiful adventure, but it can also be a little difficult to navigate, especially when relationships do not go smoothly. Even when we do not intend to, we can annoy others by accident. Miscommunications can strain relationships.

This Torah portion spells out many religious rituals. Why are there so many to perform? Turns out these rituals are easy to perform correctly; consistent ethical behavior can be more difficult. Lighting Shabbat candles is much easier than properly managing many aspects of our lives.

The feelings created by prayer during rituals can be much more meaningful to us than those evoked by regular words. Prayer gives us a chance to be consciously grateful for the blessings and gifts we often take for granted. Prayer also helps us to focus privately on strengthening our weaknesses, to reinforce and rededicate ourselves to change.

Daily we perform the routines of bathing, reading, and exercising because we know the benefits these bring. These rituals infuse physical, mental, or spiritual growth into our lives. Are we open to new religious routines that can strengthen areas of our lives that need improvement and help us reach our goals? Regular rituals in our lives can lead to growth and help us to take on life's challenges.

—by Fred Claar

> "His offering shall be of choice flour; he shall pour oil upon it, lay frankincense on it."
>
> (Leviticus 2:1)

MAKING CONNECTIONS

- Which routines in your life are most meaningful to you?
- What areas in your life are most in need of change?
- What routines might help you master your challenges?

Daily record

You will need highlighters in three different colors. List everything you did since getting up this morning. Go back and highlight in one color everything that is a daily task or ritual. In a second color highlight anything involving prayer, journal writing, meditation, or other spiritual activity. Use a third color to highlight time spent with friends or family. What did you learn? What color would you like to see more of? Why?

VAYIKRA

"Thnx God!!!"

"You shall bring . . . your grain offering of first fruits."
(Leviticus 2:14)

When we want to express gratitude to a friend, relative, or associate, we have the opportunity to take some time and communicate one-on-one. We can text, tweet, or actually write a thank-you note. We need to compose a thoughtful message, make it personal, and show effort. People really appreciate our efforts to say thanks.

In Torah portion *Vayikra*, God commands the Israelites to donate the first fruits of their harvest to the Temple. Though the Israelites work hard all year to grow their crops and wait anxiously to see the fruits of their labor, they are required to give away their best produce instead of enjoying it themselves. Donating their first fruits to the Temple is an expression of gratitude for all the goodness in their lives.

Putting ourselves out to make another person feel good is worth the effort. Like the Israelites, we too have much to be thankful for in our lives. The way we sincerely recognize and thank those people whom we care about and who care about us represents a gift of our time, thought, and effort. The next time you have the urge to quickly type THNX!!!, consider taking a few extra moments to express your appreciation more slowly and thoughtfully. The fruits of your labor will be greatly appreciated in return.

—*by Rabbi Yael Hammerman*

MAKING CONNECTIONS

- What three things are you most thankful for in your life?
- How do you express your gratitude to others?
- Have you ever written a thank-you note? Have you ever received a thank-you note? What did it say? How did it make you feel?
- If you could write a thank-you note to God, what would it say?

Thank-you cards

Choose a special person to whom you would like to send a thank-you note. It can be for anything. Spend some time decorating cards and writing the notes together.

Feeling Grateful

Sometimes it's easier to see flaws around us or within ourselves than to recognize how many of the ordinary parts of our lives work well. Acknowledging what is working is at the heart of feeling gratitude, and gratitude is central to affirming all we have and all others do for us. Gratitude is key to a feeling of well-being and consciousness of the many blessings in our lives.

In Torah portion *Tzav*, the Israelites express their thanks by bringing an offering to the Temple of an animal or grain. Something concrete is offered to show gratitude. In the Torah, gratitude is an integral part of spiritual life.

We too can nurture this feeling in ourselves by stopping for a few moments each day and thinking of all the things we have for which to be grateful. When we do so, we become conscious of our blessings and feel enriched. It is also a good habit to encourage in our friends and family members. It's important to cultivate this awareness and to sincerely say thank you. In this way we can form a lifelong habit of feeling and being grateful for the many blessings we have.

—*by Rabbi Dianne Cohler-Esses*

> "He offers it for thanksgiving."
> (Leviticus 7:12)

MAKING CONNECTIONS

- What are things for which you feel grateful?
- What are some ways to show gratitude?
- What concrete offering might you give to show your gratitude?
- How can we learn to appreciate ourselves and those around us more?

Alphabet gratitude

Write a list of things you are grateful for, one for each letter of the alphabet. Or go around the circle and take turns saying what you are grateful for, starting from A and going through Z.

TZAV

Humility versus Insecurity

> "He shall take off his vestments and put on ordinary clothes and carry the ashes outside the camp."
>
> (Leviticus 6:4)

Humility is a difficult trait to teach and to acquire. We must understand the difference between humility and insecurity. Insecurity is a lack of confidence in our abilities. Humility is achieved when we have confidence in ourselves along with awareness that our abilities are in fact unmerited gifts that come with responsibilities.

The Torah portion *Tzav* contains a reminder to the priests that they are there to serve with humility. Priests perform their Temple rituals in magnificent dress, but they must regularly perform very menial tasks, such as cleaning the altar, in ordinary worker's clothes.

The priests, the most noble and sacred group in the nation, are thus constantly aware that they are to serve with humility.

There's a perpetual tension between developing a strong sense of self and ensuring that we don't become self-centered and egotistical. We must remember that we are all part of a larger picture. The larger picture is our family, our community, our country, our world, and our universe. As we grow, so should our appreciation of the vast contributions others have made to our well-being, and this should develop our sense of awe and humility.

—*by Rabbi Moshe Becker*

MAKING CONNECTIONS

- Who are some high achievers who appear to be humble?
- Can a person be very good at something and be humble at the same time?
- Is there something very good or wrong with a high priest taking out the garbage?
- Can a healthy sense of humility contribute to self-confidence?

Human sculpture

Work in groups of four or five to make a human sculpture. It can be moving or still, with people holding each other's weight or simply attached to one another in some way. Have each small group present its sculpture before the whole group. How was each person a necessary part of the whole? How did you feel about your part in the group sculpture?

Constantly Feeding Our Internal Spark

Tzav

Jewish learning is a continuous process of discovering the richness and relevance of our tradition. Many people think learning can stop when school stops. Stopping Jewish studies after age thirteen is all too common.

This Torah portion, *Tzav*, instructs that a small fire must burn permanently on the altar, representing the desire within each of us to connect to something bigger and higher, just as a fire always reaches upward. This small flame also reminds each of us that we have a spark inside us of yearning to learn and improve. It is our responsibility to nurture our spark by feeding it through continued learning.

The smallest commitment today to Jewish learning and knowledge can feed a blaze for generations. Our books, texts, and traditions bring new meaning to us at different stages of our lives. An easy way to restart our Jewish journey is to visit www.myjewishlearning.com and explore its rich treasures of information. Consider signing up for one or more of their special-interest weekly e-mails. Jewish tradition is sustained by our passion for constant learning.

—by Rabbi Moshe Becker

> "The fire on the altar shall be kept burning."
> (Leviticus 6:5)

MAKING CONNECTIONS

- Did you know that the brilliance and wisdom of the Torah's values/ethics are available to everyone, nonbeliever or believer? Why would people who don't believe in God still study Torah?
- What societies have been positively affected by the Torah?
- What are some examples of Jewish wisdom that is relevant to everyone's life today?
- What are some ways you can incorporate Jewish learning into your routine?

Everyone is a teacher

Ask participants to choose something they would like to teach about Judaism for one minute. Give at least fifteen to thirty minutes of preparation time for the one-minute lessons.

You Are What You Eat

We all need to eat and feed our families. But how we do so involves many small decisions. Think about being in a supermarket; we all make numerous decisions on every shopping trip concerning the food we buy. We are inundated by products and need to make decisions based on various factors such as healthfulness or what appeals to our family.

In this Torah portion, we are told very specifically that we cannot eat whatever we want whenever we want. Discipline, in Judaism, is an important part of eating. According to the Torah, following the discipline of what we can eat and what we can't eat makes us holy. The complex rules from Jewish tradition for keeping kosher teach discipline, requiring us to think carefully about our food choices. Making these choices teaches us that food and eating are sacred matters.

While some of us may choose to keep kosher and some may not, it's important to keep in mind that making wise choices about the food we eat elevates the act of eating. Families eating healthful food together are involved in a sacred activity—taking in the bounty of the earth. Consider what would elevate your eating experience into one that consciously acknowledges the blessings that are abundant at your dining room or kitchen table.

—by Rabbi Dianne Cohler-Esses

MAKING CONNECTIONS

- What kinds of foods do you like to eat?
- Do you know where these foods come from?
- Which kinds of foods make you feel good when you eat them?
- Why is it important to eat together with your family?
- What is the value of applying discipline to what we eat?

Field trip

Visit a community garden, community-supported agriculture farm, or food bank in your community. Learn about their efforts to bring fresh food to your community.

Actions Have Consequences

In the 1600s, Sir Isaac Newton taught that for every action in the physical world, there is an equal and opposite reaction. For example, if you press a button with your finger, your finger is also pressed by that button. (Try it!) Newton's principle not only applies to the physical world; it applies to many areas of our own lives as well. Every action we take produces a reaction. Our actions have consequences.

Centuries before Newton's discovery of the laws of motion, Aaron's sons learn this lesson the hard way in this Torah portion. They perform a ritual not commanded by God and are instantly very severely punished. The Torah portion is teaching us that our actions can have important and immediate consequences.

Life brings both good and bad consequences, depending on our actions. Sometimes we can predict what the consequences may be. For example, if we hit our baby sister, she will probably cry. If we buy our mother flowers, she will probably give us a big hug and kiss. If we don't study, we probably won't do well on the test. Sometimes, though, we cannot tell what the consequences of our actions will be. We just have to trust that if we make the right choices, good consequences will follow.

—by Rabbi Yael Hammerman

> "They offered before Adonai alien fire, which God had not enjoined upon them."
> (Leviticus 10:1)

MAKING CONNECTIONS

- Did you ever do something without first thinking about the consequences for yourself or for others? What happened?
- Can you think of a time when your actions had either negative or positive consequences? How did you feel? What did you learn from the experience?
- Have you ever predicted the consequences of your actions and been surprised by a different outcome?

Natural and logical consequences

Talk about natural consequences and logical consequences. I drop a plate. The natural consequence is that it breaks. The logical consequence is that I have to clean it up. Have participants get into pairs. Each pair lists five actions that have natural or logical consequences, either actions they have done or that they make up. Each pair shares the list with the group, and the group has to guess what the natural or logical consequence is.

Reason Gets Lost in Anger

> "He [Moses] was angry with Eleazar and Ithamar."
>
> (Leviticus 10:16)

We can behave rashly when we are angry. Anger clouds our reason, and we may accuse others unjustly. It can be difficult to remember what good motivation another person may have for his or her actions. Though we may have reason to be upset, often our emotions blind us to the other side of the situation.

In this *parashah*, Moses gets angry with Eleazar and Ithamar, two of his nephews. He thinks that they have done something wrong, and he loudly scolds them. But their father Aaron interrupts Moses and explains that his sons have not actually done anything wrong. Their way of doing things was acceptable, too. In his anger, Moses had lost his reason and ability to consider the situation. In the end, he is humbled and relents.

Moses's anger clouds his reason, and his nephews suffer. How many times have we exploded at someone, missing their good intentions and reasonable explanations because of our anger? We are not alone in our efforts to calm down so that we can see clearly. Like Moses and Aaron, we can rely on our friends and loved ones to help us calm down when we are upset and not lose our rational selves to anger.

—*by Rabbi Judith Greenberg*

MAKING CONNECTIONS

- Why is it so hard to give others the benefit of the doubt when you are angry?
- When you look back at a time you had an angry outburst, how do you feel? Would you react differently now?
- How can you help someone calm down when he or she is angry?

Calm-down sandwich

You will need colored paper in brown, beige, green, and red, plus sandwich bags. Cut out two slices of brown "bread," two slices of beige "meat" or "cheese," a slice of red "tomato," and one of green "lettuce." On the top piece of "bread" write "Calm-Down Sandwich" along with your name. On the bottom piece of "bread," copy a soothing song or poem. On the meat or cheese, lettuce, and tomato pages, write ideas of things that help you calm down when you are angry. Keep your sandwich in a sandwich bag to look at when you are angry.

How to Use Your Most Powerful Weapon

Everyone is born with a powerful weapon, which can be used for both good and evil. This weapon grows over time but remains small and mostly concealed. It's bumpy, pink, and slippery but can be pulled out and put away in a blink of an eye. This weapon is your tongue. Your tongue is used to create thousands of words every day, and each word has the power to harm or to heal. We are defined by how we use our tongues and by the words that leave our lips each day.

This Torah portion, *Tazria*, teaches us about the strength of words. The ancient sages believed that the skin disease described in this portion was a punishment for slander and spreading malicious gossip. By gossiping, people can hurt others' reputations and make them appear poorly in public.

In return, the rabbis believed, slanderers would be punished with a skin disease that causes them to appear poorly before others.

While today we know that diseases are not caused by words, words are like arrows. Once unleashed, they cannot be withdrawn. Like arrows, words have the ability to pierce those with whom they come in contact. We must be careful with our most precious weapons, our tongues, and the words they create.

—*by Rabbi Yael Hammerman*

> "The priest shall pronounce him impure."
> (Leviticus 13:8)

MAKING CONNECTIONS

- When have your words hurt someone else? How did you feel after saying something hurtful?
- When have another person's words hurt you? How did it feel?
- How can you use your words to help others?

Speech fast

Ta'anit dibur, a fast from speaking, is a Jewish tradition. Practice speaking as little as possible for one hour or one day. Tell your close friends and family you are practicing this. Use smiles and gestures to communicate, and use words only when absolutely necessary. Then report about your experience. How did it feel?

TAZRIA

The Power of Words

> "It shall be reported to Aaron the priest."
>
> (Leviticus 13:2)

Words that are used to hurt others also harm the speaker. When people gossip, certainly the person gossiped about is hurt, but the person listening and the person doing the gossiping are also damaged. But our words can also be used for good, to help build people up instead of to break them down.

According to the rabbinic interpretation of Numbers, chapter 12, along with this Torah portion, Miriam was punished with leprosy for speaking ill of her brother Moses. While we might not break into boils when we gossip or spread rumors, doing so certainly can make us ugly on the inside.

There is a story that is often told about the dangers of gossip: A woman spreads untruths about a neighbor in her village. When she wants to make amends, she approaches an elder in the community, tells him how sorry she is, and asks what she can do to apologize. He brings her to the top of a hill on a windy day with a pillowcase full of feathers. He instructs her to open the pillowcase, and the feathers fly everywhere. He then asks her to collect the far-flung feathers. She protests, saying that it is impossible to track down each feather. He responds that so too is it impossible to undo the damage that gossip causes, for each piece of gossip told catches the wind and travels far, just like the feathers.

—by Rabbi Kerrith Rosenbaum

MAKING CONNECTIONS

- Have you ever participated in spreading gossip?
- What effect did it have on the person it was about?
- What effect did it have on you?
- What would you do differently if you had the chance?

Not listening to gossip

Break into small groups of three or four. One person is assigned to be the gossiper. Other group members practice modeling what to do to stop the gossip from continuing. You can use direct speech, body language, or action to stop the gossiper. Now switch roles. Make sure everyone gets a turn at being a "gossip stopper." Talk about how it feels. Are you afraid of losing friends or being labeled if you try to stop gossip?

Creating Your World through Language

Just as the world was created through language in Genesis, we all create our personal worlds every day through speech. We can both create and destroy with words. We can hurt other people through speaking negatively about them. Speaking about people behind their back, we can harm reputations and thereby even harm friendships and businesses. In our social and interdependent world, reputation is at the heart of one's status both personally and professionally.

Jewish tradition is particularly sensitive to the power of speech and how it can be damaging. Rabbinic commentary on this Torah portion addresses the consequences caused by speaking negatively about others, an act that is called *lashon hara*, or "evil talk." It includes slander, gossip, and other kinds of destructive language.

Think for a moment about your family: How do siblings talk about one another? How does your family talk (or not talk) about neighbors? We may believe that this kind of speech in our families is internal and therefore harmless. However, how we speak at home is a model for how we speak outside our homes. The less we use negative speech at home, the less likely we will use it outside.

—*by Rabbi Dianne Cohler-Esses*

> "The priest shall make atonement for him before Adonai."
> (Leviticus 14:18)

MAKING CONNECTIONS

- Why is it important not to say negative things about others?
- How do you feel when you find out someone has said something negative about you?
- Why do you think people like to gossip and find it so appealing?
- What might help you to engage in it less?

What's happening in this picture?

Bring in some images that show people interacting in different settings, such as police speaking to citizens, people talking to each other, or scenes of schools or playgrounds. Have participants work in small groups to come up with a positive and a negative scenario for each picture. How different are the ideas you came up with? Can we tell by looking what is really happening? Can you see how rumors get started?

M'TZORA

Attitude Shows What Is Happening Inside

"I inflict an eruptive plague upon a house."
(Leviticus 14:34)

Attitude is crucial to living well. For both children and adults, the attitude we have has a lot to do with how we experience our life as well as how we experience one another. For example, how we approach our required tasks each day is important. If we approach them with dread and resentment as opposed to acceptance and relative good cheer, we communicate negativity to ourselves and others.

This *parashah* is about a skin disease called *tzara'at*. Some commentators see this skin disease as a result of spiritual illness, an external growth that signifies what is amiss inside. It is kind of a mirror in which what you look like reflects who you are.

Today, people no longer actually suffer from this disease. Nor do people in our culture generally believe that our appearances are afflicted when we suffer from spiritual illness. But perhaps attitude, as opposed to our appearance, is the external signifier of what's happening inside. Reflecting on our approach to life and our daily attitude is a good way to begin exploring the state of our spiritual health.

—*by Rabbi Dianne Cohler-Esses*

MAKING CONNECTIONS

- What are the things you have to do every day?
- Make a list of which things you like most, which least, and why.
- How would you describe your attitude toward the things you have to do?
- What can you do in your daily life to make the tasks that you like least more enjoyable?

Affirmations

Many people believe that telling yourself positive affirmations can affect your attitude. Write down four to five affirmations, positive statements that express how you would like to feel about yourself and your life. (Some examples: I have lots of energy. I am succeeding in my schoolwork. I care about other people.) Practice repeating each statement ten times. Do this every day for a week and report back to the group. Did your attitude change?

86

Scapegoating

> "Thus the goat shall carry on it all their iniquities to an inaccessible region."
>
> (Leviticus 16:22)

Blaming others is a human tendency. How much easier it is to place responsibility on another's shoulders than to accept responsibility for our actions! We like to shift the weight of our own flaws and misdeeds on to another, especially when we have not lived up to our own or others' expectations. When confronted with our own behavior, we may find ourselves saying things like "He started it!" or "It was her fault!"

The Torah portion *Acharei Mot* describes the original scapegoat. The high priest confesses the sins of Israel while placing his hands on a goat, which is then sent out into the desert as part of the atonement process. The original scapegoat symbolically carried away the misdeeds of Israel. Today, we use the term "scapegoating" to refer to an individual or group who blames another person or group for their own flaws.

This Torah portion serves as an important directive. The goat lightens the load of Israel's sins in an overall process of forgiveness. While we are to take responsibility for our own actions, there has to be room for a lightening of the load of our errors through forgiveness. We have to be able to start over, which is what this Yom Kippur ritual is all about.

—*by Rabbi Dianne Cohler-Esses*

MAKING CONNECTIONS

- Do you ever blame others for your own mistakes? Why or why not?
- Do others ever blame you for their mistakes? How does that feel?
- What makes owning up to our own faults and flaws so difficult?
- How has scapegoating hurt people and societies?

Rock painting

Collect rocks for your group in advance or as part of the activity. Paint two rocks (with paint or colored pencils), one to show qualities and behaviors you want to keep and one with qualities and behaviors you want to let go of. Use words or colors to represent the qualities. Take the "scaperocks" to a stream, beach, or gravel pit and let them go together. Take the other rocks home to keep.

ACHAREI MOT

Food Choices

"For the life of all flesh—its blood is its life."

(Leviticus 17:14)

When we think about food, it has become popular to ask, "Do you live to eat, or do you eat to live?" Our feelings about food and the choices we make about eating say a lot about who we are as people.

This Torah portion, *Acharei Mot*, contains many rules about the food we eat that are incorporated into our modern system of keeping kosher. There are rules about the types of foods we eat, about how we prepare those foods, and even about when we eat them. The Torah text connects food to the idea of holiness, which might lead us to ask what is holy about food.

It is easy to understand what it means to "eat to live." We know that we need to take in a certain amount of food to provide energy and keep us healthy. We can also imagine what it means to "live to eat," to take great pleasure in ingredients, recipes, and cuisine. But what does it mean to think about our food choices in terms of holiness? What would it look like for us to make food decisions based on our ethics and values? This could mean the discipline of eating organically or locally, being vegetarian, or keeping kosher. There are lots of ways we can change the way we make our decisions about food, but most important is that we raise our awareness about what we consume.

—by Rabbi Kerrith Rosenbaum

MAKING CONNECTIONS

- Where do you fall on the "eat to live" versus "live to eat" spectrum?
- What do you think about when you decide what to eat?
- Are there any special limitations on choices you make (e.g., vegetarian, gluten-free)? If so, why?
- How do you think your food choices impact the world?

Learn about your food

Explore some cutting-edge thinking about food and food supply by choosing a video from the video library at changefood.org. View the video as a group, and make a list of questions. Seek out a food expert in your area to talk to you more about where your food comes from and how your food choices can make a difference.

Say No to Revenge and Grudges

K'DOSHIM

We can find plenty of reasons to hold a grudge or seek revenge. Is it worth it? Some say yes and are energized by animosity to others. Most people, however, realize the futility and burden of carrying grudges. Letting go of slights, insults, and bad behavior of others benefits us. Rabbi Hillel has a great image for us. When challenged to explain the entire Torah on one foot, he responded, "What is hateful to you, do not do to another. The rest is commentary, now go study."

This Torah portion teaches us not to bear a grudge or take revenge on others and is directly followed by probably the Torah's most famous line, "Love your neighbor as yourself." Deep down we know that may be challenging, but it is nonetheless a worthy goal.

We easily excuse our own bad behavior when we are tired, annoyed, or distracted. Shouldn't we be as charitable in judging others? When we bear a grudge or take revenge, we do not allow other people to say they are sorry and fix their mistakes. We do not give them the chance to try again. Wouldn't we want to be given another chance? Rabbi Hillel's on-one-foot image of treating others as we wish to be treated can serve as an important reminder.

"You shall not take vengeance or bear a grudge. . . . Love your neighbor as yourself."
(Leviticus 19:18)

—by Rabbi Yael Hammerman

MAKING CONNECTIONS

- What does it mean to love others as you love yourself? How can you do this?
- Can you think of a time when you held a grudge or took revenge? How did it make you feel? How do you think the other person felt?
- How would you explain the Torah while standing on one foot? Try it out!

On-one-foot speeches

In small groups, practice taking turns standing on one foot and explaining what you think are the most important life lessons. Time yourselves and see who can combine balancing and talking for the longest. What do you learn from trying to sum up important truths "on one foot"?

K'DOSHIM

The Holiness of Our Bodies

> "You shall not make gashes in your flesh."
> (Leviticus 19:28)

It can be difficult in our society to have a sense of respect and acceptance for our own bodies, with all their inherent differences. Women especially are often held to impossible standards when it comes to body weight and appearance. Eating disorders abound, mostly for girls, but also among boys. Boys and girls, men and women, become obsessive about weight and appearance, and the importance of bodily appearance can, unfortunately, overshadow other life interests and relationships.

In this Torah portion, there is a law against making gashes in one's flesh and also against tattooing oneself. We are commanded to be holy, and one of the ways we become so is by treating the body as sacred, not permanently marring it in anyway. No matter what its size, shape, or appearance, the body, just as it is, is considered holy.

How can we counteract some of society's messages, which place so much emphasis on the body as object? Using the Torah's concept of the body as holy, we can present an important alternative. By placing emphasis on caring for one's body through healthful eating, bathing, and exercising, we can show that a sense of bodily sanctity can be nurtured. We can communicate to others struggling with body-image issues that they are acceptable, even holy, just as they are.

—by Rabbi Dianne Cohler-Esses

MAKING CONNECTIONS

- What are the best ways to take care of your body?
- Why do you think people made gashes in their bodies in ancient times? Why do they do it today?
- Do you know anyone who has tried to harm their body? How can you help them?
- How does bathing or making healthy food choices contribute to our sense of the holiness of our bodies?

Mirror

What goes on in your head when you look in the mirror? If possible, get a few mirrors. Work in pairs, and practice standing in front of a mirror and saying positive things to yourself. The job of the partner is to encourage the person to come up with positive statements about the reflection in the mirror.

Gleanings from Our Own Blessings

It's easy to look up the street and see that the grass is a little greener at the homes of neighbors. Maybe they have a new car or are wearing the newest fashions you wish you could have. It's often much harder to look the other way, down the street or, perhaps, across town, to see how your grass might look greener to so many others. Your car may not be the newest, but it's a solid, safe car that runs; you have the clothes and food you need. Though it may be hard to see at times, we all have abundant blessings, and even a surplus.

As we think about finding small surpluses, let us turn to this Torah portion, *K'doshim*. Here we learn how to harvest our fields. We are told to leave the corners unharvested, and we are told that we cannot go back to collect any produce that we dropped along the way. We learn that we leave this produce in our fields so that those less fortunate—those without fields of their own—will have food to eat and a little livelihood. It is remarkable that there is no minimum-size field for leaving this gleaning; the assumption is that any landowner can always spare a little.

This lesson from the Torah helps us to look at what we have and see the corners we could leave unharvested. Can we donate barely used outgrown clothes or sports equipment? Can we forgo a new purchase and give a little more to those who are less fortunate? Or how about putting a few extra cans in the cart at the grocery store each visit, saving up our own gleanings for a food bank?

—*by Rabbi Judith Greenberg*

> "When you reap the harvest of your land, you shall not reap all the way."
>
> (Leviticus 19:9)

MAKING CONNECTIONS

- Where do you have a surplus in your life?
- How might you use this surplus to help others?
- How can you make sure to see the abundance of your blessings?

Food drive

Collect unopened dry food items from your class or community. Make and share a list of most useful items. Visit the food bank where you are delivering the food and learn more about what they do in the community.

Managing Our Anger

"You shall not profane My holy name."
(Leviticus 22:32)

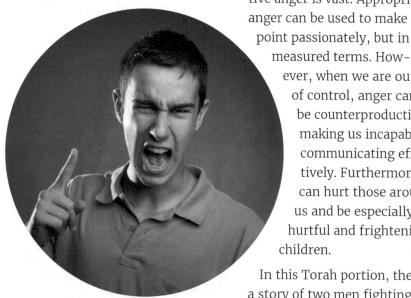

Everyone gets angry at one time or another. But the difference between purposeful, productive anger and destructive anger is vast. Appropriate anger can be used to make a point passionately, but in measured terms. However, when we are out of control, anger can be counterproductive, making us incapable of communicating effectively. Furthermore, it can hurt those around us and be especially hurtful and frightening to children.

In this Torah portion, there is a story of two men fighting with one another. One is so angry that he curses the other, using God's name in vain. The Torah makes clear that cursing, even when one does so in the course of anger, is not permissible. Anger doesn't excuse destructive behavior.

We might commit many destructive acts when we are angry. We might throw things, slam doors, or curse. However, when possible, controlling anger in a measured and purposeful way is the best way to model good communication. The best way to control anger is to think about what the point of the anger is before acting. We can then make a conscious decision concerning whether getting angry is the best course of action for the situation at hand.

—by Rabbi Dianne Cohler-Esses

MAKING CONNECTIONS

- What makes you angry?
- What do you do when you get angry?
- How do you feel when someone else gets angry?
- What are the best ways to manage your anger?
- Have you ever accomplished anything lasting in anger?

Numerical arguments

Pair up and have an argument. Instead of using words, you can only say numbers. Argue as loudly and persuasively as you want, but don't use any words. See how long you can keep the number argument going without laughing. Conclude by watching Monty Python's classic sketch "The Argument Clinic."

Kindness to Animals

We spend a lot of time reminding ourselves how important it is to be kind to one another. We speak about seeing each person's humanity and treating others the way that we would want to be treated. But what happens when that "other" is not a person but an animal? Respect for the living creatures in this world is also an important value.

This Torah portion includes laws about treating animals properly. The very fact that these laws exist says a lot about Judaism's appreciation of the role of animals in our lives. Humans and animals both deserve to be treated with dignity. The Torah is teaching us to be sensitive to the animals we encounter in our lives.

In the theme song from the 1967 musical *You're a Good Man, Charlie Brown*, Charlie's friends list all of the things they like about him. One line reads, "You are kind to all the animals and every little bird." Being kind to animals can make us better humans. We can measure ourselves by the way we treat the world around us, and animals are part of that world.

—*by Rabbi Kerrith Rosenbaum*

"When an ox, sheep, or goat is born, it shall stay seven days with its mother."

(Leviticus 22:27)

MAKING CONNECTIONS

- What role do animals play in your life?
- How have you been kind to or helped an animal?
- Can you think of an example where an animal is kind to or helps a human?

Visit an animal shelter

Visit a local animal shelter and find out more about what they do and what kind of help and donations they need.

EMOR

"You shall live in booths [for] seven days."
(Leviticus 23:42)

Hospitality

The ability to give to others is a great blessing. Hosting guests and taking care of them is an important way to express this. Guests care much more about your attitude toward them than the expense or beauty of the surroundings.

This Torah portion, *Emor*, discusses Jewish holidays. We are called upon to celebrate these holidays joyously and always instructed to make sure we share the joy with others, with our families as well as guests we invite into our homes. In fact, we are taught that taking care of a guest's needs takes precedence over one's relationship with God.

We have so many great gifts, and we should enjoy them fully.

Our gift of the ability to make others happy and to give to them allows us, briefly, to be "godlike." Our own enjoyment of the world is incomplete if we cannot share it with others. Make the effort to have an open home and bring others into your world.

—*by Rabbi Moshe Becker*

MAKING CONNECTIONS

- What makes you comfortable in a home, no matter how humble?
- Discuss the difference between entertaining and hosting, my party versus the guests' needs.
- What sacrifices are you willing to make to have a guest? What are you not willing to do?

Hosting

Make a meal together and invite guests. Divide up the tasks of menu planning, shopping, cooking, setup, and cleanup. Review the event after it is over. What did you enjoy about it?

Words Can Hurt

"Sticks and stones can break my bones, but names can never hurt me." This ditty, often recited by someone who is called names, is designed to protect us from the meanness of others. But, words, truth be told, are powerful weapons. Indeed, it would be more honest to chant, "Sticks and stones can break my bones, but names can hurt me!" Sensitive people can be especially vulnerable to the words of another.

In this Torah portion, we are enjoined, "You shall not wrong one another," which is understood in rabbinic tradition to mean not to hurt one another with words or in other ways. Instead we are to consider the effect of our word choices and their impact on others. The Jewish tradition places great emphasis on not hurting another's feelings.

It's important to model the appropriate use of language by being considerate of others' feelings. Harsh words and tone can hurt more often than we realize. Our words can backfire, causing damage to relationships. Firm but kind words can be much more effective than yelling, no matter what a person has done.

—by Rabbi Dianne Cohler-Esses

> ## "You shall not wrong one another."
> (Leviticus 25:14)

MAKING CONNECTIONS

- Has anyone ever called you a name or hurt you with the words the person used?
- How did you respond?
- Have you ever hurt someone else with the words you've used? What other words do you think you could have chosen?
- How can we learn to communicate with positive language?

Learning to use "I" statements

Work on this activity in pairs. Think of a situation where someone really upset you. Write down what you wanted to say to them in anger. Now look over what you wrote and change all your statements to first person. Using "I" statements avoids putting people down and helps you own your own feelings. Example: "You broke that dish. How could you do that?" "I" statement: "I really loved that dish. I am sad that it is broken." Take turns practicing, with each person doing a few examples. How might "I" statements improve your communication during conflict?

B'HAR

Not Misrepresenting

> "When you sell property to your neighbor or buy . . . you shall not wrong one another."
>
> (Leviticus 25:14)

Judaism is concerned with the ethics of our everyday actions, even those that are seemingly harmless. For example, you walk into a store to get information about buying an item that you have no intention of buying in that store. You ask the proprietor all kinds of questions. Afterward you go home and buy the item online for a better price. You weren't doing anything wrong, just being an educated consumer, right? Wrong! According to Jewish law you misrepresented yourself, acting as if you were a potential customer and falsely getting the salesperson's hopes up. One is only allowed to compare prices if one has the intention of possibly purchasing the item.

According to Torah portion *B'har*, we should not "misrepresent" ourselves. This is more subtle than lying. There are many ways to create a false impression. To take a seemingly benign example, imagine that people assume you keep kosher and you do not. You do not contradict them because you feel that puts you in a better light. However, your lack of speaking up creates a false impression and deceives them.

This is a very demanding standard of honesty. We are expected to act according to the truth of our intentions and identity. Except when play-acting, we are not meant to pretend to be who we are not, actively or passively. Relationships with others can only be real if they rest on honest assumptions. Being truthful about ourselves is a habit we must cultivate.

—*by Rabbi Dianne Cohler-Esses*

MAKING CONNECTIONS

- Do you ever pretend to be something you're not or allow others to believe something about you that is not true? Why or why not?
- How do you think your friends would describe the real you? Is that really who you are?

Analyzing advertising

Learning activities for analyzing advertising are available online. Encourage participants to share examples of ads they like or dislike. What are the overt and covert messages of the ad? Do you think the ad misrepresents the product? Why or why not?

Sharing Is Letting Go of Control

Some people need to be in the driver's seat. Some reign over the kitchen as their personal kingdom, while others refuse to hand over the TV remote. It can be hard to relinquish control, in the car and at home, at work and in school. We all take part in power struggles, vying to get our way and be in charge. What does it take to loosen our grip and share control?

This Torah portion, *B'har*, teaches us an important lesson about letting go of control. Every seven years land and indentured servants must be released. The Torah is legislating away slavery and being "green" by giving land a year of rest from planting and harvesting.

Above the crack on the Liberty Bell are words found in this Torah portion: "Proclaim liberty throughout all the land, unto all its inhabitants!" (Leviticus 25:10). How can we bring this lesson into our homes? While it may be impossible to "proclaim liberty throughout the home, unto all its inhabitants" without creating too many fissures in the family, we can start small, beginning with sharing control over the car, in the kitchen, and with the TV remote and other items. Letting go is hard work, but loosening our grip will ultimately make us feel freer.

—*by Rabbi Yael Hammerman*

> "In the seventh year the land shall have a sabbath of complete rest."
> (Leviticus 25:4)

MAKING CONNECTIONS

- What's the difference between losing control and loosening your control?
- When is being in control a good thing, and when do we benefit from sharing power?
- It has been more than 250 years since the Liberty Bell was inscribed. Has liberty been given to all the inhabitants of the land? How can you help make this ideal a reality?

Giveaway

Arrange a giveaway in your group or community. Ask everyone to bring something to give away. You can have a theme, like books, toys, or clothes. Arrange to donate the leftover items to an organization in your area.

B'CHUKOTAI

Sharing the Wealth

"All tithes from the land . . . are Adonai's."
(Leviticus 27:30)

Most Americans have warm homes and enough to eat, and their children have toys to play with. And yet, there are many people here in America and around the world who don't have enough. Some of those people we pass on the street each day. Others may be living in the margins, in substandard housing or in shelters.

In this Torah portion, we learn about tithing. Tithing is a structured way to give to those who don't have enough. It means that you give a tenth of whatever you have to others who are needy. Another manner of giving described is leaving the corners of one's field, so that the poor can come

and harvest with dignity. While the Torah mandates giving, it mandates an amount that is reasonable to give away—one that leaves us with more than enough—so that we are more likely to fulfill the command of giving to the needy.

It's important to develop a lifelong habit of giving. We can do this through giving tzedakah, through helping out at soup kitchens or food banks, or through finding ways to serve the needy in our community. These actions can help us develop a deep sense of responsibility to others.

—by Rabbi Dianne Cohler-Esses

MAKING CONNECTIONS

- What do you think our responsibilities are to those who have less than we do?
- How can you give? Which of your things could you give away or share?
- How does it make you feel when you help out someone else?

Tzedakah drive

Choose a worthy organization near your home to support. Collect from your group, and involve others if appropriate. Make part of your effort learning more about the organization and how it helps people in your community.

Rules

We have all sorts of rules in our lives. Some are serious, make sense, and are easy to follow, while others are more difficult to obey. Rules vary greatly, from "don't run into traffic" to "don't copy a friend's homework." Some are more universal rules like "do not steal," and some are household rules like "trash gets taken out on Thursday night." Some are very clear in how to obey them, such as "do not murder," and some are more open to interpretation, such as "be kind to others." Why do we choose to follow rules? Is it because we are afraid of the consequences or because we believe in the rules themselves?

The question is at the heart of this Torah portion, *B'chukotai.* All Israelites are instructed to follow rules for the betterment of themselves and society. It is each person's choice to follow the rules; however, there are consequences when rules are broken.

We follow many rules every day, but we also break some. How is it that we decide which ones fall into each category? Do you always follow the "rules" of a nutritious diet or the "laws" of recycling? When you follow or break a rule, is it because of your feelings about the consequences of breaking the rule or the reward of following it? Ultimately, we navigate our way through many decisions each day, and no matter what our choices are, it is important to think about why we are making them.

—*by Rabbi Kerrith Rosenbaum*

> "If you follow My laws and faithfully observe My commandments . . ."
> (Leviticus 26:3)

MAKING CONNECTIONS

- What are some rules that are easy to follow? Why are they easy?
- What are some rules that are harder to follow? Why are they hard?
- Do you think about the consequences when you are thinking about a rule?
- What is an example of a rule that you follow because you believe in it?

Debate

Have a debate about whether the saying "Rules are made to be broken" is correct. Divide into two groups. Each side must research and present its case.

NUMBERS
B'MIDBAR בְּמִדְבַּר

Torah Topics

Appreciating Boredom

"Adonai spoke to Moses in the wilderness."
(Numbers 1:1)

We may hate what we think is boring. However, much of what's important in life is not fun-filled and exciting. While many of our days can be interesting (one hopes!), some parts of school, like memorizing facts, are simply rote. Family life can be fun, but chores often are not. There are plenty of highs and lows in life, but most of life falls right in between.

The Torah portion begins the fourth book of the Bible, Numbers. It starts the tale of the Israelites' wandering through the wilderness. They have already been through the excitement of escaping from Egypt and receiving the Torah at Sinai. Now, they are simply traipsing through the desert, as they will be for the next forty years. But the Israelite journey through the desert is more than just wandering. It is a time for testing limits, for growth and renewal. It is a time for consolidating their identity as a nation and their relationship with God.

It's important to appreciate the "boring" moments of life. In working through boredom we can learn patience and fortitude, two important character traits. When we complain of being bored, there may not be an immediate exciting solution. Instead, we may need to work out the "problem" of boredom for ourselves. By figuring out what to do about being bored, we can find what's valuable in the less exciting moments of life.

—by Rabbi Dianne Cohler-Esses

MAKING CONNECTIONS

- What do you find boring?
- What do you do when you are bored? Does whining or complaining help?
- Why might it be important to be bored sometimes?

Bored jar

Make your own "bored jar" and decorate it. Fill it with little slips of paper listing ideas of what you can do when you are bored. Make sure activities that help others find their way into the jar. Next time you are bored, pull out an idea and try it!

Order versus Disorder

Our lives are busy, and in our rush to get things done, we risk expending unnecessary energy. When there is little time, what can we do to make sure that we are still creating meaningful moments and maximizing our potential? One way to do that is to create order and build rituals into our everyday lives.

In this Torah portion, *B'midbar*, the Israelites do just that. When traveling in the desert, they need to set up their camps. This is no small feat, since they must organize so many different things, among them the people, the tents, and the Ark itself. They manage this by creating a ritual for setting up the camp. This is not a religious ritual, but rather a system put in place to help manage day-to-day events.

Ritual is important in our lives. Whether setting aside time to have dinner as a family, implementing a system to manage the morning rush, or knowing that Wednesday night dinner is spaghetti, when we build order into our lives, we begin to manage the seemingly overwhelming tasks. We can take comfort in knowing that there are some things that will remain constant in our hurried lives. Rituals can ground us, adding a sense of calm, and they can also push us, giving us a structure to help us manage all that we take on.

—*by Rabbi Kerrith Rosenbaum*

> "The Israelites shall encamp troop by troop."
> (Numbers 1:52)

MAKING CONNECTIONS

- What is a daily or family ritual that helps you?
- Is there a daily or family ritual you would like to create?
- Do you have routines that get you through the week?
- What is one area of your life in which being more organized would help you to succeed?

Spring cleaning

Pick a part of your home, school, or community space that you would like to work on organizing. Work together or separately. Set a timer for one hour and see what you have accomplished. If you work separately, report to the group on your organizing activity. Talk about the benefits of having organized this space.

Learning from Adversity

> "So they marched,
> each with his clan
> according to his
> ancestral house."
>
> (Numbers 2:34)

A mother hovers over her young son climbing on monkey bars. A girl's parents won't let her walk alone to the school bus stop two blocks away. Another parent decides what her children wear to school each day. Of course parents have the job of protecting their kids, but the question is how much protection is needed. Challenges bring growth and help us to develop our full potential.

The name of this Torah portion, *B'midbar*, means "In the Wilderness." The children of Israel wander around the wilderness for forty years, a journey to the Promised Land that should take just a few weeks. But the children of Israel were slaves for four hundred years, and they need to grow out of their slave consciousness in order to have the maturity to create an ethical society in the land of Canaan. They need to face the obstacles and challenges of the desert. At times they have no food or water. They lose confidence in their leader. They face battles and are terrified. They often yearn to go back to Egypt, where they felt secure. But before they become ready to fulfill their dreams, they need to face themselves in the wilderness and grow up as a people.

We also need to learn to face ourselves, and at times having to face things alone teaches us something we cannot learn any other way. Everyone must learn how to make decisions and how to deal with conflicts. Parents can help and of course should be consulted if the situation is dangerous or abusive. For our maximum development, we need to venture out on our own, sometimes failing and sometimes succeeding.

—by Rabbi Dianne Cohler-Esses

MAKING CONNECTIONS

- What do you think you can do for yourself, and when do you need a parent's help?
- How have you dealt with obstacles or failures in the past? What might help you in the future?
- What makes you feel stronger inside?

First aid or babysitting course

Arrange a first aid or babysitting course for your group. Learning skills you need makes it possible to face challenges independently. Online versions of these courses are also available.

When the Green-Eyed Monster Visits

Jealousy is a powerful force. Sometimes it is natural to feel jealous of friends: "He has the more expensive sneakers"; "She has straight hair"; "He's taller than I am"; "She's a faster runner."

In this Torah portion, a husband is jealous and suspects his wife of infidelity. The Torah goes to great lengths to set out an elaborate procedure aimed at allaying his jealousy. In this way, the Torah acknowledges what a destructive force jealousy can be.

We can all work to try to curb jealousy in ourselves. We can try to refrain from comparing ourselves to our friends and neighbors. By focusing on what we have, rather than on what others are and have, we can live more happily. Rabbinic wisdom declares, "Who is rich? One who is happy with what he has."

—by Rabbi Dianne Cohler-Esses

> "A fit of jealousy comes over him."
> (Numbers 5:14)

MAKING CONNECTIONS

- What makes you jealous?
- What do you think might help you to be less so?
- Has jealousy ever prompted you to say or do something that you regret?
- Can we learn from our jealousy?

Mirror/selfie fast

Jealousy happens when we are focused on ourselves, usually when we are afraid we will lose something we have or not get something we want. Spend twenty-four hours without looking in the mirror or taking selfies. Use this time to cultivate a sense of who you are inside and how you relate to others. Report back to the group what you learned from this experience. Did avoiding looking at yourself change how you see others?

NASO

Mistakes Make Great Lessons

> "When a man or woman commits any wrong toward a fellow man . . ."
>
> (Numbers 5:6)

Everyone makes mistakes. It's natural to try to run from mistakes, hope nobody notices or makes a fuss, and move on. In reality, though, our mistakes are precious opportunities. They give us insight into life and ourselves, allowing us to become stronger by learning to avoid the same pitfalls in the future.

In this Torah portion, *Naso*, we learn about the comeback process after making a big mistake. The verse introduces the topic with the words "When a man or woman . . . ," not "If a man or woman. . . ." This teaches that mistakes are a built-in feature of life. When they happen, there is the opportunity for an acknowledgment of error and a process of improvement.

We like to think of ourselves as good people, which we usually are. That doesn't mean we're perfect though. Life is a journey of growth and development, and we can only grow if we know where we need improvement. A mistake supplies that piece of the puzzle. Our mistakes teach us what not to do in the future and shine a light on character traits we can improve. Sometimes they can be funny, too!

—by Rabbi Moshe Becker

MAKING CONNECTIONS

- Did you ever learn something from a mistake? What did you learn?
- Have you ever made the same really bad mistake twice? Why or why not?
- How can we use our mistakes as learning opportunities?

Monitoring self-talk

Take a piece of paper and write down the things you usually say to yourself when you make a mistake. Look them over. Are they negative or positive? Cross out each negative comment and replace it with a positive one, if possible using a different color pen or pencil. For example, "I am so dumb" can be replaced with "Everyone makes mistakes. My mistake is an opportunity to learn." Share what you learned with the group.

Role Models

Parents are models for their children. For better or worse, children learn how to be in the world from their parents. From our parents we learn that it's not what we instruct verbally, but what we do ourselves that is the most powerful teacher of all.

In this Torah portion, the laws of a Nazirite are enumerated, for someone who voluntarily takes on stringent rules for a defined period of time, abstaining from wine, cutting hair, and contact with the dead. Samson was an example of a Nazirite, whose goal was to achieve a higher-than-required level of holiness.

The example of the Nazirite discipline can lead us to reflect on what we can take on voluntarily to be better ethical and spiritual models. For example, we might think of refraining from speaking ill of our neighbors, friends, and family, of committing to a greater level of honesty, or of volunteering to do social justice work. It's important to choose a few specific areas and set achievable goals. We don't want to create the illusion that we are perfect. That can only lead to disappointment and disillusionment. It's important to be honest about our weaknesses even as we try to model our strengths. We can all find areas for improvement.

—by Rabbi Dianne Cohler-Esses

> "He shall not drink vinegar of wine or of any other intoxicant."
> (Numbers 6:3)

MAKING CONNECTIONS

- From whom do you learn? Who are your heroes and role models?
- What do you learn from them?
- What areas of your life would you like to improve?

Spiritual role models

Ask each person to bring in a quote from a spiritual role model. Talk about why you chose these role models and these quotes. How do they inspire you?

Leadership: Bringing Out the Best in Others

> "Would that all Adonai's people were prophets, that Adonai put God's spirit upon them!"
>
> (Numbers 11:29)

Being a good leader at work and at home is a difficult task. But being a good leader does not mean necessarily that we are in control. It may mean being the one who promotes the strengths of others. The problem is that often when we see others' strengths, we feel threatened. We think their strengths mean the diminishment of our own. It's either "they have the power" or "I have the power." Sharing leadership is a real challenge.

In this Torah portion, it is reported to Moses that two men are prophesying in the camp. Instead of being threatened, Moses welcomes them. He says, "Would that all Adonai's people were prophets!" (Numbers 11:29). Moses, supreme prophet and leader that he is, recognizes that sharing power is the best kind of leadership. A leader should encourage and facilitate leadership in others.

Teachers, parents, and mentors who celebrate the successes of those they lead are cherished. When we are given the opportunity to lead, we can strive to act like Moses and to welcome others to share leadership. The best kind of leaders are those who promote leadership in others.

—by Rabbi Dianne Cohler-Esses

MAKING CONNECTIONS

- What qualities are essential in a leader?
- When and how do you act like a leader?
- Is it harder for you to be a leader or a follower? Why?

Leadership game

The leader sits in a chair facing one other person. The rest of the team sits behind the second person. The leader can communicate only with the second person and only in writing. The second person can communicate with the whole team but only with gestures. No talking is allowed. The leader is given a card with a question on it about the team (for example: Who on the team has a winter birthday? Who has the most pets? How many team members have been to Disney World?). The leader has two minutes to get this information. Play the game with different people taking turns being the leader, the second person, and team members. Discuss what you learned about leadership and communication.

Appreciating What You Have

"There is nothing at all! Nothing but this manna to look to!"
(Numbers 11:6)

No matter how blessed we are, it is always easy to see someone who has more, has achieved more, or has something that we want. In a world where very little is still private, TV shows give tours of huge estates, newspapers and magazines report annual salaries, and various social networks show us others' accomplishments. It can be hard to live without looking over our shoulder to see who has more than we do. However, it is just as important to look over your other shoulder and see those who have less.

In this Torah portion, the Israelites are in the desert and hunger for meat. They complain that the manna, though tasty and sustaining, is not enough. They have not yet learned to be thankful for what they have.

There will always be those who have more than we do and those who have less. The challenge is to be happy with our portion, to be thankful for what we do have. An important part of being content is to stop comparing ourselves to others. This does not mean that we cannot be ambitious or work hard to achieve, but our work must be done thoughtfully and with gratitude for what we already have.

—by Rabbi Kerrith Rosenbaum

MAKING CONNECTIONS

- Do you ever wish for something you don't have? What is it, and why do you want it?
- What are some of the things in your life that you are thankful for?
- How do you show your gratitude?

Book and game swap

Organize a book and game swap for your group, school, or community. Organize the books and toys by age. You can make this into a tzedakah activity by charging an entrance fee and donating the funds raised to an organization that helps the needy. Find out where you can donate the leftover books and toys as well.

Igniting Curiosity's Flame

> "Let the seven lamps give light."
> (Numbers 8:2)

Seeing a young child smile can light up our world. Children are naturally curious, and their faces light up with understanding and delight. We need to keep encouraging and nurturing that curiosity in ourselves and others. Asking questions and looking for answers nurtures our natural curiosity. This is true education as we use resources to follow our own curiosity into deeper understanding.

This Torah portion describes the seven lamps that light up the sanctuary. The lamps can be seen as a metaphor for education, the way we light up our hearts and minds. Education is not only a matter of school and academic learning. We explore the world in all kinds of ways, with our bodies, our souls, and our minds. It's important to encourage our own natural abilities and ways of discovering the world.

Education is about lifelong habits of questioning and exploring. Our own Jewish sources illustrate traditions of questioning and responding to those questions over generations. You are invited to join the Jewish conversation with your own questions and thoughts about things like God, the Jewish people, and Jewish rituals.

—by Rabbi Dianne Cohler-Esses

MAKING CONNECTIONS

- What are you most curious about?
- How do you go about finding out things?
- What other ways might you find the answers you are looking for?
- How does it feel to learn new interesting information?

Mini-research project

Pick a Jewish topic that interests you. Write down your questions about that topic. Talk to a parent, teacher, or rabbi about how to find out the answers, and spend at least one hour trying to find some answers to your questions. Then share what you learned.

Self-Confidence Makes Courage Possible

Courage is necessary to get through certain moments in each of our lives. For some, it takes courage to meet new people or walk into a party alone. For others, a job interview or moving to a new place requires courage. There are those who have an abundance of courage and those who have it in short supply. But what makes courage possible is self-confidence—a positive self-image and a belief that things will turn out all right.

In this Torah portion, Moses chooses twelve leaders to go to the Promised Land to see whether it is conquerable and inhabitable. Ten of them come back saying that it's not possible to conquer the land because they perceive that giants live there. Two of them, Joshua and Caleb, come back saying, "We can do it." They are ready to go forward. The ten men who lack courage see themselves as very small, saying they are as "grasshoppers" in their own eyes and in the eyes of the inhabitants of the land. They lack the self-confidence it takes to do what is required.

To have a positive self-image, we need encouragement. We need others who support our efforts at trying new things and meeting new people. Whether it is the first day at a new school or skiing for the first time, courage and a positive self-image are needed to get through frightening moments.

—*by Rabbi Dianne Cohler-Esses*

> "We looked like grasshoppers to ourselves, and so we must have looked to them."
> (Numbers 13:33)

MAKING CONNECTIONS

- Where do you think courage originates?
- Are there times you can think of when you wish you had more courage?
- Where do you think self-confidence originates?
- Is there a difference between courage and self-confidence? What is it?

Courage collage

Make a collage about courage. Find images or words that show your definition of courage. This can be done as a group or individual project. When the collages are completed, ask participants to share and explain the images they chose and/or make a display or exhibit of the collages.

SHLACH L'CHA

Keeping Things in Perspective

> "The whole community broke into loud cries, and the people wept that night."
>
> (Numbers 14:1)

Mishaps can happen to anyone. Whether it's stubbing your toe as you get out of bed in the morning or forgetting your lunch at home, we all have our share of annoyances and challenges. The trick is to make sure we stay in charge of our reactions and do not let a small mishap escalate to a full-blown crisis.

This Torah portion, *Shlach L'cha*, recounts the story of the twelve scouts sent by Moses to check out the Land of Israel as the people of Israel drew closer. Ten spies gave a very unfavorable report. In fact, they seemed to have perceived everything they saw negatively. This attitude rubbed off on the nation; instead of making a realistic evaluation of the report and planning accordingly, the people mourned and lamented the fate they were sure awaited them. Their reaction brought about the tragic result of unnecessarily lengthening their stay in the desert by thirty-nine years.

We all "mess up" occasionally. Sometimes we say the wrong word to people at the wrong time and offend them. We can dig in deeper and get upset at the other person's reaction, or we can take control of the situation and apologize properly. Mistakes and mishaps happen, but we are responsible for our reactions and can ensure that a small mishap remains nothing more than a small bump along the journey of life.

—by Rabbi Moshe Becker

MAKING CONNECTIONS

- Give one example of a minor annoyance or mishap and one example of a major crisis or tragedy.
- In what way should your reaction be different in the two situations?
- Why is it bad to "make a mountain out of a molehill"?

Analyzing a picture

Bring in one or two photographs or painted images. Each picture should have multiple elements and some abstract or nature images. Ask participants to write a short paragraph about what they see in the picture. Have participants read their paragraph and talk about the different perspectives they illustrate. Talk about how different people perceive the same scene differently. How is it possible to adjust our perceptions on a regular basis?

Courage to Think Differently

"Have no fear then of the people of the country."
(Numbers 14:9)

Most likely you have found yourself in a group situation where your opinion simply does not match the group consensus. Do you speak your mind, or do you keep silent? If you choose to share your opinion, how do you go about introducing it? And if you remain quiet, do you think of it as being for the "good of the group"?

In this Torah portion, *Shlach L'cha*, a group of scouts is sent out to report back on that land that the Israelites are about to enter. When the twelve scouts return, ten of them paint a dire picture. But Caleb and Joshua speak out positively against the report of the ten.

It can be difficult when we find ourselves with a different point of view from that of a larger group. Our tradition teaches us that the majority opinion is not the only one that matters. In fact, in the Talmud when there are lengthy debates that finally resolve, the text goes to great length to document the dissenting parties' names and their minority opinions as well as the majority opinion. It can take a lot of strength to stand up for what you believe in, but it can be important. In fact, you are likely to find that if you share a differing opinion, others start to speak up as well. Diversity of thought leads to interesting conversations, creative solutions, and new possibilities.

—by Rabbi Kerrith Rosenbaum

MAKING CONNECTIONS

- Can you describe an incident in which you held a different opinion from a group?
- Did you share it? Why or why not?
- How do you feel when someone in a group introduces a new perspective?

Pop-ups

Have different members of your group take turns leading this. Sit in a circle. Ask everyone to stand who has a pet, who has a grandparent from another country, who likes spinach, and so on. Each leader should choose at least four pop-ups. Discuss what you learned about differences. How did it feel being the one who was different?

KORACH

Rebellion

> "You have gone
> too far!"
> (Numbers 16:3)

Teens often rebel against their parents, and parents may react immediately and angrily. Parents and teens can become involved in a reflexive pattern of action and reaction, without any reflection to help them understand each other. Perhaps a child is testing limits or feels that the limits placed on him or her are no longer appropriate for his or her age. Perhaps parents are afraid of what will happen if their child has more freedom.

In this Torah portion, *Korach*, a group rebels against the leadership of Moses and Aaron. Korach and his followers ask: Why are they in charge? Isn't everyone sufficiently holy to lead this congregation through the desert? Moses's first reaction is an interesting one. He does not immediately defend himself and Aaron. Rather he takes a few minutes to reflect before responding. Can we also learn to pause and take a moment to figure out how to respond before reacting?

The next time you are in a family argument, try to stop for just a moment. This can productively interrupt what might be a habitual chain reaction. Rather than reacting, think about what is really going on here and what specific response might be called for. Might it be better to discuss this when you are calmer? Is it time for compromise or for exploring what's going on with the other person? Like Moses, stop to consider your best response, and see if you can learn more about the conflict you are in and how best to resolve it.

—by Rabbi Dianne Cohler-Esses

....

MAKING CONNECTIONS

- When you are feeling very angry about something, how can counting to ten before talking be helpful?
- What are some other techniques that stop arguments from escalating?
- How do you feel when an argument escalates to heated words or slamming doors?

Journal entry

Write about a conflict in which you were recently involved. What did you want? What happened? Were you afraid of something? Did you get what you wanted? If not, how did you respond? How might you have responded differently? If you feel comfortable, share about what you wrote with a partner or with the group.

Jealousy Makes Us Foolish

KORACH

Jealousy is resentment against another's success or advantage. There is almost always a deeper, inner insecurity that is causing the jealousy. Jealousy is not automatic. When we are feeling insecure, jealousy can be triggered.

In this Torah portion, *Korach*, there is dissension among the ranks while the Israelites are wandering in the desert. The source of the tension is the way one group sees Moses and Aaron. Korach and his followers believe that Moses and Aaron have taken too much of the leadership upon themselves. We may wonder, what was truly behind the men's feelings? We find our answer just a little further in the text. Korach and his followers ask: If everyone is holy, then why are Moses and Aaron singled out among them?

The answer does not really matter to them, because their jealousy clouds their ability to think rationally, and no amount of explanation calms their emotions. It is easy to get worked up about things that seem unfair, especially if they are highlighting dissatisfactions in our own lives. If we allow our emotions to take over and we lose rational thought, then our actions can spin out of control. On the other hand, if we are able to identify these feelings in ourselves, we can tap into them in a thoughtful way and try to handle things calmly and logically.

—by Rabbi Kerrith Rosenbaum

> "Why then do you raise yourselves above Adonai's congregation?"
> (Numbers 16:3)

MAKING CONNECTIONS

- What events or circumstances make you jealous?
- What do these events trigger inside you?
- What are some ways you can manage those feelings?
- Can you think of a time jealousy kept you from being rational? What happened?

Analyzing leadership

Think of leaders you admire. Brainstorm together a list of characteristics that make these leaders suited to leadership. Make another list of sacrifices that leaders have to make to maintain their positions. Are you jealous of leaders? Is leadership something to which you aspire? Why or why not?

KORACH

Renewing a Relationship

"Moses sent for Dathan and Abiram, . . . but they said, 'We will not come!'"
(Numbers 16:12)

What happens when you find yourself in a disagreement with someone? Sometimes a distance grows that must be bridged in order to save the relationship. When that moment arrives, who will be the person who reaches out and extends the olive branch? Is reaching out to the other person first a sign of strength or a sign of weakness?

On one hand, it takes a lot of character to attempt to reconcile with someone when the relationship is not going well. On the other hand, reaching out may be seen as "giving in" or not holding strong to your point of view.

In this Torah portion, we see Moses model the first approach. Korach and some followers rebel against Moses and Aaron. As things get heated in the community, Moses decides to reach out to some of the rebels and asks them to meet with him in order to open lines of communication.

Does it matter whether they came or not? In this case, they did not. However, that should have no effect on the initial decision to reach out. For that step to reopen communication says much more about the one who asks than it does about the person who receives the request. Reaching out can be seen as brave because if no one reaches out, there is no chance to communicate, to work things out, or to move forward. Reaching out is a risk that comes with a big potential reward, the renewing of a relationship.

—by Rabbi Kerrith Rosenbaum

MAKING CONNECTIONS

- Is reaching out to reconcile a sign of strength or weakness? What does it take to reach out?
- Can you describe a time when you reached out to someone?
- Can you describe a time when someone reached out to you?
- What do you do when you reach out and the other person does not respond?

Practicing reconciliation

Work in pairs. Make a list of opening lines you can use when you want to reconcile with someone with whom you are in conflict. Practice saying the lines out loud. How does it feel to try to reconcile?

When We Lose Control

People lose control at times. We may get excessively angry and behave impulsively or destructively. We may scream and yell, eat too much, or act out in other ways. The reasons for such behavior are many. Sometimes there is something missing in our lives, a hole we don't know how to fill, or a difficult issue we don't know how to address. That darkness lurks and then suddenly, when we least expect it, erupts into unwanted behavior.

In this Torah portion, Moses loses control. The people are complaining about lack of water in the desert. God tells Moses to speak to a rock in order to draw water from it. Instead Moses hits the rock in anger. He loses patience with his people, who are constantly complaining. But there is also a backdrop of loss to Moses's behavior. His beloved sister Miriam has just died. Moses's grief causes him to be short on patience.

It is important that we learn healthy ways of coping with our feelings. All people lose their temper sometimes, and learning healthy ways of coping with frustration, worry, and tension can help us deal with issues before they build up into an explosion. We need to be sure that we do not use destructive behaviors such as overeating, smoking, or alcohol and drugs to cope with feelings or ongoing frustrations. Addressing deeper issues head-on is always better than lashing out or acting out.

—by Rabbi Dianne Cohler-Esses

> "Moses raised his hand and struck the rock twice with his rod."
> (Numbers 20:11)

MAKING CONNECTIONS

- What kind of situations might lead you to lose your temper?
- What happens when you lose your temper? Do people around you get hurt?
- How else do you handle difficult problems in school or at home?
- What are some of your healthy coping mechanisms?

H.A.L.T. poster

H.A.L.T. stands for "Hungry, Angry, Lonely, or Tired." Any of these states can make it easier for us to explode and lose control. Make a poster using words or faces to depict how these things look or feel to you. Add suggestions in words or pictures for positive responses to these situations.

CHUKAT

Bullying and Name-Calling

"Moses and Aaron assembled the congregation in front of the rock."

(Numbers 20:10)

Often people label entire groups as "weird," "bad," or "uncool." Sometimes kids join cliques or engage in a kind of social warfare at school, with one group pitted against another. This can even lead to bullying or gang violence. Even if we don't go so far as to join a gang or hate group, it is a challenge not to be judgmental and to be open to others.

In this Torah portion, *Chukat*, the children of Israel are traveling through the desert when their beloved leader Miriam dies. Then there is no water for the community. They complain to Moses, saying, "Why did you make us leave Egypt to bring us to this wretched place?" (Numbers 20:5). God tells Moses to speak to the rock to draw forth water from it. Instead, Moses angrily hits the rock, saying, "Listen, you rebels, shall we get water for you out of this rock?" (Numbers 20:10). In his anger, Moses uses a destructive label for his people, calling them rebels in public.

How can we cultivate an attitude of openness to others? Rather than rejecting others for how they dress or how they behave, we can practice showing tolerance and respect for others despite their shortcomings. By being vigilant about not labeling and judging others, we can over time develop a healthy respect for those who are different from us, rather than putting others down in order to raise up our own self-worth.

—by Rabbi Dianne Cohler-Esses

MAKING CONNECTIONS

- How is social life at your school organized? Do some kids publicly reject others?
- Is there ever name-calling at school? Bullying? How should we respond to such behavior?
- What can we do proactively to make sure all kids are included?

Bingo

Make bingo sheets with a chart of sixteen squares. In each square write a challenge: "Find someone who has a pet"; "Find someone who has moved more than once"; "Find someone whose favorite color is green"; etc. Leave at least one square for participants to fill in themselves. See how fast you can find a different person who has a different experience. Then talk about how difference is an important part of life and the value of being part of diverse groups and communities.

Words Matter

"Sticks and stones can break my bones, but words will never hurt me." Every child knows this popular aphorism, but the sad truth is that words do matter and they can hurt. When we feel stressed, angry, or frustrated, many of us speak without thinking first. Words can become daggers that wound others as well as ourselves.

In this Torah portion, *Chukat*, Moses is asked to provide water for the Israelites. Just before the water flows from a rock, Moses, apparently worn out by the demands of leadership, loses his temper. Moses calls his people "you rebels" and, in exasperation, strikes the rock twice. In light of this shocking behavior, God immediately decides that new leadership is needed to bring the people into the Land of Israel.

This painful biblical episode shows how all people need to be careful with their words, especially people in positions of authority. Harsh words can cut a little deeper and last a little longer when they come from someone we respect, trust, and love. That is precisely why we need to be careful, not just about what we do, but also about what we say. Just as words can push people apart, so too can they bring us closer. By taking the time to think before we speak, we have a better chance of finding the right words in every situation.

—by Rabbi Charles E. Savenor

"Listen, you rebels, shall we get water for you out of this rock?"

(Numbers 20:10)

....

MAKING CONNECTIONS

- What can we do to make sure that we think before we speak?
- How do we respond when someone hurts our feelings with words?
- When have someone's words of encouragement helped you?
- Water can keep us alive or drown us, and fire can warm us or destroy us. How are words similar to water and fire?

Learn a prayer

At the end of every Amidah, we say a prayer that begins, "God, guard my tongue from evil." Find this prayer in a siddur, and take some time to learn the prayer together. What parts of the prayer appeal to you? Why do you think we conclude all our prayers with this prayer? Do you know any good tunes to it?

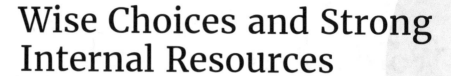

Wise Choices and Strong Internal Resources

BALAK

> "Please do not refuse to come to me. I will reward you richly."
> (Numbers 22:16–17)

Endless choices face us each day, relatively casual choices like what to eat for dinner, and ones that are more profound, such as "should I tell the truth in this situation?" At times we have a strong feeling about the right choice in a given situation, but because of undue pressure from family or friends, we may make a different decision. For teens, peer pressure can be very strong and can lead to decisions that are not wise or morally sound.

In this Torah portion, much pressure is put on a non-Israelite prophet, Balaam, to curse the Israelites. God gives explicit instructions to the prophet, telling him that he cannot curse the Israelites. However, Balaam seems tempted by the riches and honor that he will receive from the king of Moab if he curses them. Balaam ultimately discovers that he doesn't have the power to curse the Israelites. He only has the power to bless them, according to God's will.

To stand up against peer pressure, we must have strong internal resources. Making difficult choices may result in others not liking us or misunderstanding our actions. It is difficult to take such risks, and we may be worried about what will happen if we alienate our friends. We need to develop strong inner resources and learn to trust ourselves and our intuition, rather than only seeking friends' approval.

—*by Rabbi Dianne Cohler-Esses*

MAKING CONNECTIONS

- What are some difficult decisions you've had to make? What happened as a result of those decisions?
- How do you know which decisions are good and which are not correct for you?
- Who is a person you can speak to who helps you make good decisions?

Role-play

Role-play some of the difficult decisions you discussed or other situations of peer pressure such as kids trying to get their friends to go along to a party where alcohol is being served, or kids trying to pressure other kids into stealing something. Practice being in the role of saying no. How does it feel?

Temptations

It is hard to resist temptation. To do so, one must have a strong sense of right and wrong and be able to assess the situation rationally. Temptation exists everywhere in our world in varying degrees. Sometimes it comes in the question of an extra piece of dessert. Sometimes it is a less than honest way to get a better grade, and sometimes it takes an even more serious form. But there is always a price when we give in to temptation, and that price is transgressing one of our own values or ethics. In the case of the candy, it might be a promise to oneself to eat healthier, and in the case of the grades, it is honesty.

In this Torah portion, *Balak*, the Israelites are camped in the desert near the Midianites. The Israelites find themselves tempted by this foreign culture.

They are drawn to a foreign god, Baal-peor. They indulge their temptations, and it causes havoc in the community.

Our tradition and our lives are full of stories of temptation. People weaken for financial gain, or we become so absorbed in ourselves that we ignore people we care about. Whatever temptation lies on one end of the scale, there is a value that we hold dear on the other. It is important that we know what our values are so that we can make sure they outweigh the temptations we encounter.

—*by Rabbi Kerrith Rosenbaum*

"Thus Israel attached itself to Baal-peor, and Adonai was incensed with Israel."
(Numbers 25:3)

MAKING CONNECTIONS

- What are some things that tempt you?
- What values outweigh those temptations for you?
- What do you do to resist those temptations?

Learn about temptation

Interview two people in your life about what "resisting temptation" means to them. Take notes and report back to the group. Are there common themes in your interviews? What are some strategies the people you interviewed use to resist temptation?

BALAK

> "How fair are your tents, O Jacob, your dwellings, O Israel!"
>
> (Numbers 24:5)

Jealousy

How do you react when your friend wins a prize? A common reaction is jealousy. You may feel deficient when you see your neighbor or friend with something that you don't have. It's sometimes difficult to remember that all of us have our own set of circumstances that we need to acknowledge and accept. You may be jealous of a friend's new phone, while that person is jealous of your clothes or hair.

In this Torah portion, the Moabite king, Balak, hires a non-Jewish prophet named Balaam to curse the Jewish nation. Balaam understands that in order to curse the Jewish people, he needs to see them. He hopes that seeing them will help him to find something that will arouse the feelings of jealousy and anger he is looking for.

Jealousy is what results when we spend too much energy looking at what others have. Instead, we should be looking at ourselves and what we have, appreciating our blessings and aspiring for growth in our lives. Jealousy can paralyze us and force us to define ourselves by another person's successes. We each have unique capabilities, physically and spiritually. We need to focus on what our true potential is and work toward that.

—by Rabbi Moshe Becker

MAKING CONNECTIONS

- What are some things you wish you had?
- What are some things you are grateful you do have?
- What mind-set do you need to be genuinely happy for another's success?

Talking mirror

You can do this as a group activity with a large mirror or have small mirrors for each person. Use sticky notes or larger pieces of paper to write affirming messages such as "You are enough," "You have enough," "You are beautiful," "You are the best!" You may write any message you choose, but it must be positive. Surround the mirror with the positive messages. Next time you look in the mirror, take time to read each message.

Standing Up for Oneself

Standing up for oneself is a difficult feat. We sometimes need to stand up for ourselves to defend ourselves or to ask for things we need. Whether asking for a raise in salary or confronting a friend over a perceived hurt, standing up for ourselves means putting ourselves on the line. This can be daunting. Faced with the prospect of standing up for ourselves, we may doubt that we deserve what we are requesting, or we may wonder if we will be penalized just for asking.

In this Torah portion, there are four sisters, the daughters of Zelophehad, who have no brothers and are not eligible to inherit their father's property because they are women. They daringly stand before Moses, the priests, the chieftains, and the whole assembly and make their request to inherit their father's property. Moses confers with God and then agrees to their radical request.

We can also learn to be advocates for ourselves from an early age. It can happen on the playground or when we are being made fun of, but it may also happen in family relationships. It can be a challenge to stand up for ourselves, but it is a skill that we all need to learn.

—by Rabbi Dianne Cohler-Esses

> "They stood before Moses, Eleazar the priest, the chieftains, and the whole assembly."
> (Numbers 27:2)

MAKING CONNECTIONS

- Have you ever stood up for yourself? What happened?
- Were there times that you've wanted to stand up for yourself but you didn't have the courage? What do you think could have helped you at those times?
- How do you prepare to present your reasons when advocating for yourself?

Advocacy research

Pick a cause or issue that is important to you. Find out about someone who is an advocate for this issue. If you can, set up a time to interview that person about the issue. Or read about the individual online. Try to find out what inspires his or her courage to work for this issue.

Balancing Our Passions

> "Pinchas . . . has turned back My wrath from the Israelites by displaying among them his passion for Me."
>
> (Numbers 25:11)

Life is a series of everyday choices. Some choices are more important than others. A bagel versus cereal for breakfast probably won't make much difference, but other choices have the potential to shape the direction of our lives and the impact we make on this world. Weighty choices are often tied to the things that we are most passionate about, and when confronted with such a choice, we often use passion to help make our decision. But we must strive to find a balance between that passion and practicality.

In this passage, Pinchas sees a fellow Israelite behaving in a way that he believes to be immoral. His passion is fueled, and in his desire to right this injustice, he takes the law into his own hands. He did in fact see the man breaking a law, but was it correct for him to serve as judge and jury?

Our lives would be empty without passion. The things that we care about—the environment, sports, politics, family, and learning—add depth to our character, joy to our lives, and reasons to engage with the world. However, passion has to be tempered with reason. Sometimes our passion can drive us to take action, but sometimes we need to refrain. This balance can be difficult to achieve, yet there is great wisdom in it.

—*by Rabbi Kerrith Rosenbaum*

MAKING CONNECTIONS

- What activity or interest are you most passionate about?
- Has there been a time when your passion caused you to act when you should have stood back?
- What would have happened had you not acted?
- Have your passions changed as you have grown older?

Tug-of-war

Have an old-fashioned tug-of-war. Try to match teams evenly for strength. Encourage participants to scream and yell while trying as hard as they can to beat their opponents. Do at least a few rounds. Then talk about how it felt. Did you feel passionate about winning?

Is It Fair?

"It's not fair" is a refrain we often hear. We want rules to be applied fairly. Fairness is an ideal that is widely shared.

In this Torah portion, we learn about Zelophehad, who dies before the Jews arrive in the Land of Israel. His four daughters are concerned that his portion of the land will be lost because he had no sons. They object, saying it is unfair that women cannot inherit their father's land. Moses asks God what to do, and God decides the women's request is fair. Thousands of years ago, Jewish inheritance law changed to reflect fairness, based on the request of the daughters of Zelophehad.

Much of our engagement with the world around us arises from our sense of fairness. It is because we believe in fairness that we expect our hard work to translate into success. We often choose to step in to correct something that we believe is wrong, either by getting involved in a charitable cause or in community activism. It's our sense of fairness that motivates us to make the world a better place.

—*by Rabbi Moshe Becker*

"Let not our father's name be lost to his clan just because he had no son!"
(Numbers 27:4)

MAKING CONNECTIONS

- What is the difference between fairness and equality?
- Describe something around you that seems unfair.
- How does fairness help create a better world?

Social activism

Choose an issue of fairness that matters to you individually or to your group. It can be within your school or synagogue or in the wider community. Look for activities you can take part in (letter writing, demonstrations, fundraising), or start your own campaign to achieve fairness.

Keeping Your Word: It's Easier Said Than Done

MATOT

"If a man makes a vow . . . he must carry out all that has crossed his lips."
(Numbers 30:3)

Promises can be made easily, but keeping them is often another matter. Adults may make too many promises to children about what they can have in the future, or children may make promises to adults about behaving better. It is important to check inside ourselves about our ability to fulfill a promise before we make it. Otherwise, our words will have little value and will not be taken seriously.

This Torah portion discusses vows and the importance of not breaking a pledge. Judaism teaches not to make a verbal commitment unless you really mean it. Such a commitment is something one is morally obligated to honor, even if it later becomes inconvenient.

Over and above the seriousness of promises, there is the issue of what we say in daily discourse. It is easy to say what we do not ultimately mean. Think for a moment about how often we say no and subsequently turn it into a yes. While saying no is not exactly a promise, if we are not committed to our words, people will cease to believe us. It is important to think before we speak, not to make promises lightly, and not even to say no or yes if we don't believe that we can stand by our words.

—by Rabbi Dianne Cohler-Esses

MAKING CONNECTIONS

- Have you ever broken a promise? Why or why not?
- Has anyone ever broken a promise made to you? How did you feel?
- Do you think it is a good idea to make promises? Why or why not?

Learn about a ketubah

A ketubah is a Jewish marriage contract. It reflects the signed commitment of the parties; traditionally it lists the husband's commitments to the wife, but in more modern communities, it is a contract of mutual commitments. Find some examples of contemporary ketubot online, or ask family members to share theirs. If you have any local ketubah artists, you can invite them to share about their work.

Compromise

Family relationships are tricky. We want family members to be able to grow in their own individual ways, but we also have our own thoughts about how our family members should behave. Parents may push children to get into a school they admire or play a sport they like, even if it's not necessarily the right thing for their kid. Kids may want their parents to dress more stylishly, nag less, or care more about what the kids care about. Each family member is a unique individual with his or her own set of needs and desires.

Torah portion *Matot* relates the quandary presented by two and a half tribes of the Jewish nation. The plan was for the entire nation to cross over the Jordan River and inherit their land on its western side. This group expresses to Moses that the eastern side is the best place for their families and their wish to remain there. Moses questions them. Ultimately they make an agreement whereby the tribes can remain on the eastern side while the men from those tribes who are warriors will continue the military campaign with the rest of the nation.

Family decisions need to keep all family members in mind. Decisions parents make for children need to take the child's unique personality into account. To promote family harmony, we can strive to get to know each of our family members well, to understand their unique qualities, and sometimes be willing to forgo our own dreams to help them pursue theirs.

—*by Rabbi Moshe Becker*

"Do not move us across the Jordan."
(Numbers 32:5)

MAKING CONNECTIONS

- To what extent do your family members like the same activities as you? Is it sometimes hard to find activities you all want to do together? Why or why not?
- How does your family make compromises when it comes to family activities?

Coat of arms

Make a family coat of arms. Use a shield template and divide it into six sections. Write words or pictures in each of the six sections representing (clockwise) your name(s), your family, special talents of each member of your family, goals, motto, and the place you live. Try to include something that represents each family member, as well as the family as a whole.

MATOT

"It Wasn't Me!"

"They . . . induced the Israelites to trespass against Adonai."

(Numbers 31:16)

Picture this: Mom and dad come home and find broken glass in the kitchen, sticky juice and muddy footprints all over the floor, and no one in sight. Three kids and the dog are watching TV in the den. When the parents come in, everyone shouts, "It wasn't me!" and points across the room. Sound familiar? It's always easier to blame a younger sibling or the dog. It's less scary to point your finger at someone else than to point it at yourself.

Even Moses falls into this trap in this Torah reading. Moses accuses Israel's enemies of tempting the Israelites to sin, instead of placing the blame on the Israelites themselves.

Is it helpful to place the blame on someone else? Does accusing others fix the problem? When you claim that a mistake is someone else's fault, not only are you still left with broken glass and a sticky floor, but you have also hurt someone else's reputation and damaged your relationship. It's more complicated to improve a reputation and mend a relationship than it is to clean up the kitchen. As difficult as it can be to take responsibility for your own actions, try pointing your finger at yourself and admitting truthfully, "It's my fault."

—*by Rabbi Yael Hammerman*

MAKING CONNECTIONS

- Have you ever blamed someone else for your actions? Why?
- Have you ever been blamed for someone else's mistake? How does it feel to be accused?
- Why do we usually trust people who are consistently truthful?

Responsibility quote

Do an online search for quotes about responsibility. Find one that speaks to you. Use colored pens or pencils to write out the quote and decorate it for your bulletin board. Or make a meme that you can share with friends electronically. Make sure you include the name of the author!

Remember When...

Taking pictures and putting together photo albums is a favorite family activity. Many people enjoy looking at albums from the past and reminiscing about childhood. Remembering, however, is more than just the fun of looking at enjoyable times and how cute we used to be. Memories tell us where we come from, what we stand for, and how far we have come; they tell us which values abide over time.

In this Torah portion, Moses keeps a written record of the progress of the Israelites' wandering through the desert. Each stage of their journey is written down. In this way the Israelites can always see where they came from and how far they still have to go. They literally "know where they stand."

When parents and grandparents share memories of growing up and what they've learned along the way, everyone benefits. A sentence that starts "Remember when . . ." helps build our memories and the stories we will pass on. It's interesting to note what different family members remember. Memory is an important tool in the journey of childhood on the way to adulthood, a gauge of our lives telling us where we come from and who we are along the way. For older adults, telling stories of the past is an important part of "life review," a stage in the aging process where we make sense of our lives and the legacy we wish to pass on.

—*by Rabbi Dianne Cohler-Esses*

> "Moses recorded the starting points of their various marches as directed by Adonai."
> (Numbers 33:2)

MAKING CONNECTIONS

- What are your earliest memories?
- What is the importance of memories?
- Whom do you want to remember?
- What have you learned from family stories you have heard?

Oral history

Interview older family members about their lives and their memories. If possible, audio- or videotape them. You can also help them prepare an album, a slide-show presentation, or another visual record of their lives. If you do this as a group, you can expand the activity to include a special event for all the participants and the interviewees.

From Generation to Generation

MASEI

"Moses instructed the Israelites, saying: 'This is the land you are to receive . . . as your hereditary portion.'"
(Numbers 34:13)

Have you ever been told that you resemble a parent or grandparent? Have you heard that you sound like, think like, or act like those who came before you? Looks, attitudes, desires, feelings—all of these can be seen in families through the generations. We inherit much from those who came before us and give much to those who come after us. That may be a key to immortality; parts of our ancestors live on in us, just as parts of us will live on in our descendants.

Of the adults Moses addresses in this Torah portion, only two actually get to enter the Promised Land. The others perish in the desert and do not complete the journey to the Promised Land, a harsh reality.

How do they cope with such a disappointment? Perhaps noticing some of their own traits and desires in the younger generation gives them comfort and strength, knowing that their children will inherit their values and their love for the Promised Land.

Teachers, writers, performing artists, parents, and friends also make an impact on the next generation. From generation to generation, we pass on Jewish values, traditions, and love of Israel, ensuring their survival. Through these connections, elders become a part of the generations that follow them, and younger people benefit greatly from those who came before them.

—by Fred Claar

MAKING CONNECTIONS

- What traits and wisdom have you inherited or received from parents or grandparents?
- Which family member do you most admire?
- How does knowledge of the challenges faced by those who came before you affect you?
- How do those who came before you benefit from your maintaining Jewish traditions and love for Israel?

Scrapbook

Use a small blank book to make your own scrapbook. Ask members of your family, "What would you like to pass on to me that I should remember forever?" Write down their answers and collect messages or mementos that you or they would like to preserve, such as wedding invitations, ticket stubs, or cards. Decorate your keepsake scrapbook with family photos or symbols that are meaningful to you.

DEUTERONOMY
D'VARIM דְּבָרִים

Torah Topics

Criticism: It's Hard to Hear and Hard to Give

> "These are the words that Moses addressed to all Israel."
> (Deuteronomy 1:1)

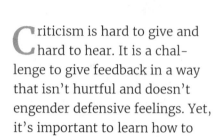

Criticism is hard to give and hard to hear. It is a challenge to give feedback in a way that isn't hurtful and doesn't engender defensive feelings. Yet, it's important to learn how to give constructive feedback, as well as to hear feedback from others.

This Torah portion begins the fifth book of the Bible, Deuteronomy. The book is in the form of a long speech by Moses given before the children of Israel enter the Promised Land. It includes a review of their history, criticism for past misdeeds, and laws meant to organize their society in the new land. This reflection on their past, their successes and failures, prepares the children of Israel to enter into the land and create their own society. In essence this is the book of their growing up and the book of instructions on how to govern. Part of that involves serious criticism.

Before you criticize another person, think first about how difficult it is to hear criticism yourself. A gentle tone and a kind word amid constructive criticism can make it possible for others to hear what you have to say without shutting down. The kindness with which we dispense feedback will make all the difference in the world to how and whether it is received.

—by Rabbi Dianne Cohler-Esses

MAKING CONNECTIONS

- How do you feel when you receive criticism from family members? From friends?
- Do you ever give others feedback or criticism? What has been the reaction from others?
- Do you think giving or receiving criticism is important?
- What is the difference between criticism and feedback?

Learn more

Learn about the SCARF model of brain-based analysis of how people respond to criticism, developed by David Rock. He uses neuroscience to explain five domains of human concern: Status, Certainty, Autonomy, Relatedness, and Fairness. Watch a video or read more about this model. How does this relate to the way we give and receive feedback in our families and schools?

The Tone of Your Voice

We have all used sarcasm at some point in our lives. It can be lighthearted or dis-respectful and mean-spirited. People on the receiving end of sarcasm are often at a loss as to how to respond to it. If the speaker is confronted, he or she often says, "I was only joking."

This Torah portion, *D'varim*, retells the story of the spies who traveled to the Promised Land and came back with a negative report to the Israelites camped in the desert. God was angry with them, not only for the negative things they said and the way they demoralized the rest of the people, but also for their tone of voice.

This teaches us that respect involves more than the words we use. The tone of our voices and our body language are also powerful vehicles of meaning. How can we model this? One strategy is to ignore sarcastic remarks. When they are not fed with the oxygen of attention, they are often extinguished. Beyond that, we can work on respectful communication at home and out in the world. There are better ways to communicate than sarcasm.

—by Rabbi Dianne Cohler-Esses

"When Adonai heard your loud complaint, God was angry."
(Deuteronomy 1:34)

MAKING CONNECTIONS

- In what kind of situations do others use sarcasm? Why?
- What response lessens the sting of another person's sarcasm?
- How are you affected by the tone of voice of others?
- Do you raise your voice to make a point? Is it effective?

Seven dwarfs tone-of-voice practice

Prepare several cards with quotes or statements. Choose seven dwarfs from your group: Happy, Grumpy, Sleepy, Sneezy, Dopey, Bashful, and Doc. Have each person read the same statement using the tone of voice of the assigned dwarf character. You can also add your own dwarfs to the mix (Whiny, Mopey, Angry, and so on). Switch around the roles and have fun with this!

Listen to All Sides

"You shall not be partial in judgment: hear out low and high alike."

(Deuteronomy 1:17)

We often jump to conclusions. We walk into a new class and quickly decide who is "cool" and who is not. We may witness an interaction between two people and immediately decide that someone is being abusive or disrespectful, even though we lack knowledge of the context. Sometimes our judgment calls are on target and sometimes they are not.

In Torah portion *D'varim*, Moses recounts the instructions he gave to the first group of judges he appointed. These instructions are repeated to remind us of their importance and timelessness. Moses emphasizes the importance of paying close attention and patiently listening to all sides. Judges must ignore external factors and do their best to learn as much as they can about the litigants and their arguments. Only then are they qualified to judge. If they can't accomplish this, they must consult with a higher-ranking judge.

We are all judges. We are hard-wired to make quick decisions about things happening around us. This is a crucial capacity, but it can also be a handicap in relationships. When it comes to other people, we must be careful to learn as much as we can about them and their circumstances before forming opinions. The "not cool" kid in the class may become your closest friend!

—*by Rabbi Moshe Becker*

MAKING CONNECTIONS

- Have you ever had your opinion of someone change after getting to know them better? Why or why not?
- Have you ever felt that others jumped to conclusions about you? How did it feel?
- Think of a situation that would look bad if a person watching doesn't know the facts. What could you do to avoid or fix such a situation?

Asking good questions

Write several dispute scenarios involving two sides on index cards or as a slide show (examples: a child says that his sibling took his toy; a student says her phone is missing and another student took it; a parent says her teenage son took the car out without permission). Working in groups of three, come up with a list of questions you would ask if you were the judges to discover the information you would need to render a verdict.

Ethics to Last a Lifetime

Raising children is not only about teaching children how to be successful in the future. It's also about teaching ethics that will carry them through their lives. The ethics we pass down to our children are meant to last a lifetime and, in fact, to outlive us.

In this Torah portion, Moses is told that he will not be able to enter the Promised Land. But he is to teach the people of Israel a body of ethics to serve them in building a new society there. This body of ethics is meant to guide the people of Israel in their new lives and into the future, into each new generation.

All Jews have a responsibility to teach our children ethics that will last them throughout their lives. Whether it's honesty, commitment, kindness to one's neighbor, giving to the poor, or gratitude, these ethics will travel into the future in the lives of our children and grandchildren. We all have the duty to teach ethics for the generations that will follow us.

—by Rabbi Dianne Cohler-Esses

> "Take to heart these instructions.... Impress them upon your children."
> (Deuteronomy 6:6–7)

....

MAKING CONNECTIONS

- What are the most important ethical teachings you have learned from your parents or grandparents?
- What do you think are the most important values in how we should treat others?
- Which lessons are hardest to remember in your day-to-day life at school or at home? Which are the easiest to remember?

Life lessons

You can share life lessons with others at any age. Imagine you are passing on life lessons to a new student entering your school, to a younger sibling or cousin, or to a creature from outer space who arrives in your town. Make a list of ten important life lessons you would pass on to this person or creature.

137

VA'ETCHANAN

Taking Care of Our Bodies

"Take utmost care and watch yourselves scrupulously."
(Deuteronomy 4:9)

Do we exercise enough? Getting enough rest, staying clean, and not smoking or using other unhealthy substances are all important ways to respect our bodies. Unfortunately, some people take better care of their fine jewelry, putting it away in velvet, than they do of themselves. Our bodies are the tools we use to realize our dreams and aspirations.

This Torah portion, *Va'etchanan*, begs us to protect and take good care of ourselves. We have so much potential within us that can only be accessed if our bodies are functioning properly. The Torah regards our bodies as "holy" objects because they are tools for doing great things.

As we journey through life, we overcome challenges. Each step along the way provides opportunities for success and spiritual growth. Our job is to make sure that we have the required physical, emotional, and spiritual reserves to meet each challenge and to take advantage of the opportunities. Caring for our bodies establishes a platform for us to shine and excel.

—by Rabbi Moshe Becker

MAKING CONNECTIONS

- What things must we do to care for our bodies?
- What happens if we don't do them?
- How are our bodies important to our lives?
- What can you do to improve your overall health?

Community walk/run

Participate together in a community walk or run. This is a great way to exercise while having fun or supporting a cause.

Facing Up to Consequences

VA'ETCHANAN

We do not always think about the potential consequences before we take action. When making big decisions, hopefully we stop to think. But when a decision doesn't seem as though it has far-reaching implications, we don't necessarily think through all possible scenarios in our minds. So what happens when we are later faced with the consequences of our actions?

In this Torah portion, we see Moses dealing with the consequences of his actions. The Israelites arrive at the Promised Land, and Moses catches only a glimpse of it. He is not allowed to enter, because of something he did in a moment of frustration while traveling in the desert, many chapters back.

How do we act when we are confronted with our actions and asked to take responsibility for them, especially when we find ourselves surprised by the unintended consequences? It is easy to be defensive and full of excuses, explaining that we didn't mean to cause harm. However, regardless of our intention, our challenge is to accept the fact that our actions brought about these consequences. There are times when apologies can begin to make things right, and there are times when, like Moses, we simply need to accept the consequences of our actions.

—*by Rabbi Kerrith Rosenbaum*

> "Let me, I pray, cross over and see the good land on the other side of the Jordan."
> (Deuteronomy 3:25)

MAKING CONNECTIONS

- When was a time you hurt someone and didn't realize it?
- How did you act when you found out?
- Have you been hurt by someone who didn't know they hurt you?
- Did you choose to tell the person, and if so, how?

Rube Goldberg machine

Make your own Rube Goldberg machine. This is a contraption that gives a physical display of how one thing leads to another. Instructions can be found online in several different formats. Or visit one on display at a local museum. Learn more about these machines and the cartoons that inspired them. What can we learn from Rube Goldberg machines about our own behavior?

EIKEV

Learning from Example

> "What does Adonai your God demand of you? . . . To walk in God's paths."
>
> (Deuteronomy 10:12)

When parents teach children, they don't only teach with words. They teach with every act they do and by sharing who they are. If a parent goes through life angry or resentful, children will learn anger and resentment. If parents go through life with love and joy, children will learn love and joy.

This Torah portion states that we should teach the words of the Torah "when you stay at home and when you are on your way, when you lie down and when you get up" (Deuteronomy 6:7). In other words, wherever we are, each and every one of our actions is a teaching moment, an educational opportunity. In fact, these words compose a part of the Sh'ma, the Jewish prayer said twice daily, as well as before bedtime and before death.

Every moment is a teaching moment, and every moment is a learning moment. Sometimes we learn who we want to be by watching how we don't want to behave. If someone packs at the last minute to go on a trip, full of anxiety and pressure, that communicates one lesson. If, however, they pack in advance and feel relaxed about the journey, that communicates another. No one can be perfect, but we all have the opportunity to model behavior for others and to choose who we want our models to be.

—by Rabbi Dianne Cohler-Esses

MAKING CONNECTIONS

- What are some of the things you learn from your parents? How do you learn these lessons?
- What do you think are some of the most important behaviors you have seen your parents and others model?
- What do you teach others through your behavior?
- What have you learned from your friends and from your brothers or sisters?

Follow the leader

This is an exercise in following another person's steps and learning nonverbally. Get together in pairs in an outside area. One person in the pair is the leader, and the other the follower. For three minutes the leader walks or moves slowly or quickly, and the follower has to imitate the leader's movements exactly. Then switch roles for another three minutes. After the walk is over, talk about what you learned by following another person's movements. Did you learn more about that person? Did you learn about yourself?

Controlling Anger

What do you do when you get angry? Slam a door? Yell at someone? Most people struggle with feelings of anger at times. We are confident that everything should be the way we want it, and when things go awry, we become insecure and angry.

This Torah portion, *Eikev*, encourages us to disavow idol worship in all its forms, even to physically destroy idols. Sometimes, though, the "idol" isn't an image or sculpture; it is ourselves. Anger is a self-centered indulgence, a modern form of idolatry.

Anger is our reaction to things not going the way we think they should. We may put ourselves and our wants on such a high pedestal that nothing else matters. I'm so sure that things should go my way that when they don't, I feel threatened and out of control. I may attempt to exercise my control over something else to compensate. I may break an object or yell at someone to regain a feeling of security. All I see is myself; my idol is what looks back at me in the mirror. It's much better to take a deep breath and calm down and to learn ways to deal with anger so that it does not get out of control.

—*by Rabbi Moshe Becker*

> "You must not bring an abhorrent thing into your house."
> (Deuteronomy 7:26)

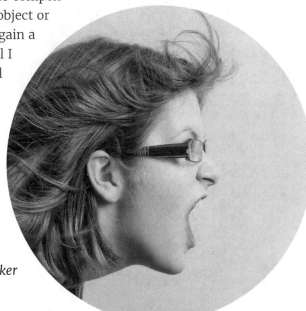

MAKING CONNECTIONS

- Talk about a few things that have made you angry.
- How could you have reacted differently?
- Is it ever good to get angry? Why or why not?
- What kinds of things can help you to calm you down?

Relaxation

Learning to relax and self-soothe is important for dealing with anger. This activity offers practice in relaxation. Have one person be the leader while everyone else lies on their backs on the floor. Practice relaxing the body, starting with the toes and going up to the head. The leader should give instructions, talking people through relaxing each part of their body. Allow three to five more minutes of silence after the leader stops talking. Then the leader should softly ask people to open their eyes and slowly sit up when they are ready.

EIKEV

Expressing Gratitude

> "When you have eaten your fill, give thanks."
> (Deuteronomy 8:10)

We lead blessed lives. Many of us have so much for which to be grateful. But it is often easy to get caught up in what we don't have and to miss the blessings amid what we feel is lacking. We may find ourselves demanding, "If only such-and-such were better in my life" or "Why can't this be easier?" Yes, it is good to be striving, but being aware of our blessings can make our lives even more blessed.

In this Torah portion, *Eikev*, Moses instructs the Israelites to be grateful for all the blessings in their lives, especially for each meal. We thank our hosts for meals, so why not thank God for making it all possible? Gratitude for what we have is a cornerstone of Judaism, and our tradition provides blessings that can remind us to be grateful for everything from our food to a rainbow.

It is disconcerting for us to see when people are not grateful for the blessings in their lives. What great blessings in our lives do we overlook because something else has gone wrong? It is easy to overlook the blessing of good health when one is healthy. It is easy to overlook the blessing of having family close by when they can get on our nerves. It is easy to overlook the blessing of a quiet evening in a busy week. Taking time to express gratitude can help us change our attitude.

—*by Rabbi Judith Greenberg*

MAKING CONNECTIONS

- Why is it hard to be grateful sometimes?
- What would make it easier for you to be grateful?
- How can you help each other notice the blessings in your lives?

Blessing after meals

Learn the blessing we say after meals (*Birkat Hamazon*) and what it means. Practice it together.

Giving to the Needy

Caring about others and giving to the needy are important lessons. However, it is easy to get caught up in our own worlds, thinking only of the things we want to buy or acquire. Sometimes giving to others takes a back seat.

The Torah is sensitive to the needs of those who have less than others and issues a mandate to help these persons. This Torah portion says that we should not harden our hearts or shut our hands in response to the needy. Charity, tzedakah, is not just a matter of feeling philanthropic, but an act of justice in our world.

There are plenty of volunteer opportunities we can participate in, whether it's building homes for the homeless, volunteering in a shelter, working in a soup kitchen, or taking part in a bake sale for earthquake relief. We can help out at blood and bone marrow drives. The more we give, whether through volunteer activities or through giving money, the more we can make this a lifetime habit and one we enjoy.

—*by Rabbi Dianne Cohler-Esses*

> "If . . . there is a needy person among you . . . do not harden your heart and shut your hand."
> (Deuteronomy 15:7)

MAKING CONNECTIONS

- Do you see poor people around you? How do you think you can help them?
- What of your things might you share with people in need?
- Have you ever volunteered to help the needy? What was that like for you?

Soup kitchen or food packing

Volunteer together at a soup kitchen or food bank. Plan in advance to spend two to three hours on this activity, and involve others in your community if you can.

Free Will and Discipline

> "See, this day I set before you blessing and curse."
> (Deuteronomy 11:26)

All parents try to discipline their children. They have different methods, but generally parents are trying to influence their children to be moral and to behave appropriately. Imposing any kind of discipline rests on the assumption that all people, including children, have free will. We can choose between good and bad behavior.

In this Torah portion, *R'eih*, Moses tells his people, "See, this day I set before you blessing and curse" (Deuteronomy 11:26). The people have a choice: they can obey the commandments and reap blessings, or they can fail to listen to the commandments and suffer. It is assumed by the Torah that good behavior leads to blessings and that people have freedom to choose and direct their own actions, even when it is difficult to control their impulses. Although we do not always see immediate good results from good behavior, we have the ability to make choices and do what is right.

Every human being has powerful impulses. We want to have fun, we want to test limits, or we want to feel that we are in control. Rewards and consequences shape our behavior over time. It works well if we have a balance between freedom and discipline. We must all learn to take responsibility for our own actions and learn how to solve problems. We all need the freedom to make our own mistakes, the freedom that allows us to discover the consequences of our actions. Through this, we develop our own self-discipline.

—by Rabbi Dianne Cohler-Esses

MAKING CONNECTIONS

- What kinds of choices are hard for you?
- What have you learned from making a poor choice?
- What helps you to make the best choices?

Taking on a discipline

Choose one discipline you would like to focus on, such as daily exercise, daily prayer or meditation, daily journaling, or a daily chore. Keep a record of your daily practice for two weeks, and report back to the group about how it goes.

Giving of Ourselves

"hat are we willing to give to help those in need?" Judaism's word for giving, *tzedakah*, translates most accurately as "justice," not "charity." We are required to give to others to create justice in our world.

This Torah portion, *R'eih*, offers some guidelines for giving in the Jewish tradition and includes the idea of tithing. Tithing is giving 10 percent of your income in money, time, or products. Even though we are encouraged to be generous in our giving, Jewish tradition teaches that we should not give more than 20 percent. The tradition is trying to model a balance between taking care of others and taking care of ourselves.

There are many ways to give and countless opportunities to make a difference. We can give money to causes or institutions that align with our values. We can work in advocacy, raising awareness and trying to promote change. We can donate food, clothing, or household goods. We can teach and educate those around us. We can serve as professional or volunteer leaders of organizations working for good in the world, and we can be involved on the most grassroots level as helpers. We can make a difference at home in private, and we can make a difference publicly in our communities. What is important is that we give graciously in relation to our means.

—by Rabbi Kerrith Rosenbaum

"There shall be no needy among you."
(Deuteronomy 15:4)

MAKING CONNECTIONS

- How can you make a positive difference in this world?
- What can you give in money, time, or items?
- How does it feel to help people in need?
- How do you avoid embarrassing someone you are trying to help?

Visiting elderly

Coordinate with your rabbi or community coordinator to connect with elders who are homebound or would like visitors. Plan a short visit, and if possible, more than one, to connect with elders in your community. Talk beforehand about conversation topics and what to expect.

"It's Not Fair!"

"You shall not judge unfairly: you shall show no partiality."
(Deuteronomy 16:19)

Small children are perpetually concerned with fairness. "It's not fair!" they cry when a sibling gets something they don't. But "it's not fair" can become something more mature as we grow older. It can become a concern for justice. It can lead to awareness that it's not right that a classmate is being teased on the playground, that a person has no place to sleep at night, or that a child does not have enough to eat.

This Torah portion urges us repeatedly to pursue justice. It is concerned that the courts are fair, that judges do not take bribes, and that the poor have the right to achieve justice as the rich do. The aim of setting up a court system is ultimately to have a just society with access to fairness for all.

We need to nurture and maintain our concern for justice. First of all, we can do the best we can to behave fairly in all situations. That can be the small beginning of coming to know what justice can mean in the wider world. Next, we can learn more about problems such as homelessness, hunger, inadequate schools, and racism and find ways to be involved in working for change.

—by Rabbi Dianne Cohler-Esses

MAKING CONNECTIONS

- What does it mean to be fair? When is something unfair?
- What do you think is the best way to deal with something when it is unfair?
- Are there situations in which being fair does not mean being equal?

Accessibility tour

Organizations that promote rights for people with disabilities sponsor "accessibility tours" where you can find out for yourself what it is like to get around your town in a wheelchair. Take a tour of your town from this point of view and find out whether equal access exists.

Will You Speak for the Trees?

D r. Seuss introduced us to *The Lorax*, his 1971 children's book that was made into a feature-length film. *The Lorax* tells the story of how the environment is destroyed by human activity and ambition. We hear the unforgettable voice of the gruff but wise Lorax, who says to the greedy Once-ler, "I speak for the trees, for the trees have no tongues!"

Like the Lorax, we too learn to speak for the trees in this Torah reading. This Torah portion, *Shoftim*, includes the commandment to protect fruit trees from destruction. Trees should not be chopped down thoughtlessly or unnecessarily. This mitzvah is the foundation for the Jewish value of *bal tashchit*, which teaches us not to be wasteful and to care for the environment.

Trees and the environment cannot protect themselves. It is up to us to guard them. Like the Lorax, we too can find ways to "speak for the trees" in our homes, schools, and workplaces. We can start by examining our daily actions. How can we be less wasteful each day? Look at the world around us. There are an infinite number of large and small ways to incorporate the value of *bal tashchit* into our lives, our community, and our world.

—*by Rabbi Yael Hammerman*

"You may eat of them, but you must not cut them down."
(Deuteronomy 20:19)

MAKING CONNECTIONS

- Think about all the things you use on a daily basis. How can you apply the mitzvah of *bal tashchit*, not being wasteful?
- How can you advocate for the environment?
- How can Shabbat be a time when your family practices *bal tashchit*?

Tree survey

Go out of your house or synagogue and examine all the trees on the property. Take note of leaves, bark, fruit, seeds, and any other aspects of each tree. You can do this activity in pairs, with each pair examining one tree. Research the trees you find to learn more about what they are and what they do. How are the trees useful to humans? You can expand this activity into a tree guide presentation or learn more about how and where you can plant trees in places that need them.

Justice

> "Justice, justice shall you pursue, that you may thrive."
> (Deuteronomy 16:20)

Our world is results oriented. We are used to productivity as a measure of what's good and right. Whether it's writing software that does what we want it to do or closing a business deal, our society celebrates the "bottom line" far more than it judges the methods used getting there.

The beginning of Torah portion *Shoftim* contains instructions for judicial proceedings. We are commanded to "pursue justice justly." Not only are the judges enjoined to focus on a just outcome, but also the litigants themselves are reminded that their pursuit of justice must be done legitimately. Justice cannot result if one party alters the facts the tiniest bit, just to make their case stronger, even if they know they are right.

Focusing on the bottom line and results is only part of the story. We need to pursue what is good and right even in the methods we use to accomplish our goals. A business transaction must be done with honesty. If there's something wrong with the house, car, or game you're selling, you must tell the buyer. Maybe this particular buyer will back out, but others will come along who'll appreciate your honesty and will be confident that now they know exactly what to expect.

—*by Rabbi Moshe Becker*

MAKING CONNECTIONS

- Why does a court always require complete evidence even if it seems obvious who is at fault?
- How do you feel when you purchase something that has been misrepresented?
- Would you be likely to shop again in a store where the truth was not told?
- How much would you trust a friend who often stretches the truth or misrepresents?

Visit a court

Visit a courtroom and learn more about how judicial proceedings are conducted in your community. Find out more about the guiding principles behind the workings of the court and the judicial system in your community.

Treating Animals with Kindness

Kindness to others can begin with treating animals with kindness. Exposure to animals can bring out our nurturing side. Time spent around animals provides an important opportunity to learn about the feelings of creatures other than human beings and can lead us to greater kindness.

This Torah portion forbids plowing with an ox and an ass together. Besides a concern for not mixing species together, plowing with an ox and an ass would be painful for the smaller animal, who would suffer in this yoking. In this way the Torah shows humanitarian concern for animals.

Learning to care for animals can bring a lot of joy. Even if you can't have a pet yourself, you can visit pet stores and zoos and learn about animals, or you could take care of someone else's a pet for the weekend. Connecting with animals can give us many opportunities for joy and learning.

—*by Rabbi Dianne Cohler-Esses*

> "You shall not plow with an ox and an ass together."
> (Deuteronomy 22:10)

MAKING CONNECTIONS

- What kind of animals do you like the best? The least?
- Have you or anyone you know ever mistreated an animal? What happened?
- Why do you think it's important to be kind to animals?

Zoo visit

Plan a trip to the zoo together. Many zoos have exciting evening or overnight activities. Spend some time observing and learning about animals that are new to you and learn more about how they are cared for and how they live in their natural habitats.

KI TEITZEI

Being Responsible for Our Actions

"Parents shall not be put to death for children, nor children be put to death for parents."
(Deuteronomy 24:16)

How can we be sensitive to being influenced by, or influencing, those close to us? Our expressed beliefs, the stories we tell, and our behavior all have an impact on families. We all know of families that have generations with the same hobbies, business interests, and views on life.

This Torah portion, *Ki Teitzei*, introduces the idea of individual responsibility. A verse from this portion states that parents shall not be punished for the actions of their children, nor shall children be punished for the actions of their parents. This was a unique idea in biblical times, a true departure from judging individuals based on the actions of their families.

It can sometimes be difficult for us to step up and take responsibility for the choices that we make because it forces us to take ownership over our decisions. It is much easier for us to say that we made a choice because of what someone else said, what we read, or what we saw. It is true that our choices are shaped by our own experiences, but they are ultimately our choices, and the Torah is telling us that we must take responsibility for our own actions.

—*by Rabbi Kerrith Rosenbaum*

MAKING CONNECTIONS

- Can you share a time that you did not take responsibility for your actions? Why didn't you? What was the result?
- Was there a time that you did take responsibility for your actions although it was difficult?
- What are some of the outside influences that help shape your choices?

Interview an elder

Interview an older member of your family or a mentor. Ask about the important choices they made in their lives and who or what influenced their decisions. Record your conversation (on video or in writing), and share what you learned.

Deceiving Ourselves

"**Y**ou can run, but you can't hide." We all have our demons, the parts of ourselves that we wish were better or we wish didn't exist within us. The best way to deal with them is to acknowledge their reality, confront them, and challenge them. Only then do we stand a chance of working them out of our system. We cannot ignore them.

This Torah portion, *Ki Teitzei*, contains a wonderful mitzvah. We are instructed to return lost objects that we may find lying in the street. Though we may be appreciative of this when we are the owner who lost the wallet, it's not always an easy mitzvah to fulfill when we're the finder. The Torah therefore reminds us, "Do not ignore it." This is a profound reminder of our obligation.

Addicts lie about their addictions, even when the truth seems obvious to the observer. Denying the reality of the addiction is an inherent part of the disease. When it comes to correcting mistakes or dealing with our issues of anger, bigotry, or even lesser things like a desire to get in shape, the first step is acknowledgment. The issue must be confronted directly. We can't look for other people or situations to blame, and we can't make excuses for mistakes. We must take ownership of the issue and tackle it. We can succeed at overcoming it. We cannot ignore it.

—*by Rabbi Moshe Becker*

"If you see your fellow's ox or sheep gone astray, do not ignore it."
(Deuteronomy 22:1)

MAKING CONNECTIONS

- Why does the Torah say not to ignore a lost object?
- Who benefits from my action when I pick up the wallet and return it?
- Give an example of something that you could choose to blame on a friend but could also take responsibility for.

"Rewriting" Torah

Study Deuteronomy chapter 22, verses 1–3 together. Put the verses into your own words as they would be written today. Are more rules needed? Which items would you include in the text? How would you rewrite these precepts for our time?

KI TAVO

Sharing What We Have

"When you have set aside in full the tenth part of your yield . . . and have given it to . . . the stranger, the orphan, and the widow . . ."

(Deuteronomy 26:12)

Many of us have an over-abundance of goodness in our lives. But sometimes in our society, with its saturation of goods and services, it is difficult to be aware of this abundance. If we have enough to eat, a place to sleep, and clothes to wear, we already have more than many people in the world. Becoming aware of how much we have, we naturally begin to think about what it means to give back to this world from which we've so plentifully received.

In this Torah portion, we are required to take a tenth of our yield and give it to those who are needy: the stranger, the orphan, and the widow. The Torah ensures that those who are needy are taken care of by their community.

Learning to give from what we have is important. We can learn to share what we have. Do you have a tzedakah (charity) box in your home and put aside something every week from allowance or income? No matter how much or how little we have, we have something to share with others.

—*by Rabbi Dianne Cohler-Esses*

MAKING CONNECTIONS

- Why do you think some people have more than others?
- What are some of the ways you can give to others?
- How do you feel when you give to others?

Toiletries drive

Collect unopened shampoos, soaps, toothpastes, new toothbrushes, and other items to donate to a shelter in your community.

Does Gratitude Come Naturally?

We have many magic moments in our families. There are times for us to appreciate our accomplishments and the people in our lives. Yet gratitude does not always come naturally. Sometimes we need a reminder: "Don't forget to say thank you!" We gain when we learn to practice gratitude.

This Torah portion, *Ki Tavo*, relates the commandments for farmers who successfully produce a new crop. The first fruits are to be brought to the Temple in a special ceremony to give the farmers an opportunity to think about their blessings and to say thank you properly.

Saying "thank you" is not just good manners. It's an attitude that must be cultivated. We need reminders to help us learn to appreciate the wonderful things in our lives and our many blessings. Jewish tradition provides blessings that we can say when we eat, drink wine, light candles, and even when we see a rainbow. These blessings help us remember to notice and be grateful for good things.

—*by Rabbi Moshe Becker*

"You shall take some of the first fruit of the soil." (Deuteronomy 26:2)

MAKING CONNECTIONS

- What blessings are in your life?
- What special gifts do you possess?
- Why should we be thankful? How should we express our thanks?
- Can one person do everything alone? What does it mean to depend on others?
- What is interdependence?

Sharing special moments

Print some photos of special moments and make them into a gratitude collage showing people and moments you are grateful for in your life. Share your collage and talk about what it represents to you.

KI TAVO

Blessings in Disguise

"All these blessings shall come upon you."
(Deuteronomy 28:2)

Imagine a parent bringing a six-month-old baby to the doctor. The mother looks on while the baby screams and squirms as the doctor pokes and pulls and gives a shot. The same baby grows up and is now a four-year-old girl at a birthday party; her mother stops her from having that final candy that she knows will make the daughter sick. Although from the child's perspective the mother may seem very mean, she is in fact acting with the greatest mercy and kindness imaginable.

Torah portion *Ki Tavo* describes a beautiful relationship between humans and God. God promises that blessing will pursue one who chooses the path of growth. But what is "blessing"? Part of the assurance of blessing here is that the blessing and goodness will "pursue us," even though we may perceive what happens to us as unfair or difficult.

Things come our way in life that don't always seem like blessings—an illness, a car accident, a disagreement. Yet we never know. An illness may be an opportunity for someone you didn't expect to show love and caring. A disagreement with a friend can be a healthy experience in your development. We can learn to be on the lookout for the hidden blessings in any situation.

—*by Rabbi Moshe Becker*

MAKING CONNECTIONS

- What makes an event or experience good or bad?
- When have you ever experienced something that seemed bad at first, but turned out to be very good?
- Why is it good to look for a benefit in everything that happens to you?

Storytelling game

Sit in a circle. The first person in the circle begins a story in which something goes wrong. The next person has to continue from that point. Halfway around the circle, the mood of the story must shift to positive, and the last person to take a turn must resolve the plot into a happy ending. The story need not be realistic. Encourage players to be as creative as possible in imagining miserable situations with happy solutions. Play a second round in reverse order so everyone gets to imagine both sides of the coin. Talk about what we can learn from these "reversals of fortune."

It Is Not beyond Reach

It's not always difficult to do something new, although it may take some effort, practice, and sometimes courage to do it. It can be difficult, though, to do something challenging, and we may need patience and perseverance.

In this Torah portion, we are told that the Torah "is not in the heavens"; in other words, what the Torah instructs is not beyond our ability to accomplish. Although much effort is required, the ethical and spiritual precepts of the Torah are eminently attainable as well as rewarding.

It is important to take on new and difficult projects at every stage of life. The new project can be as specific as learning a new instrument or as amorphous as committing oneself to an ethical precept, such as honesty. Some struggle is inherent in any accomplishment, even in adulthood. We grow and learn when we strive to achieve something important.

—*by Rabbi Dianne Cohler-Esses*

> "Surely, this Instruction . . . is not too baffling for you."
> (Deuteronomy 30:11)

MAKING CONNECTIONS

- What new thing would you like to try?
- What things, if any, are you afraid to try?
- What makes it difficult to try something new?
- Have you ever found something to be worth the effort even though you could not fully accomplish what you wanted?

Obstacle course

Work together to create your own obstacle course in an outdoor or indoor space. Work to make it challenging. Give each person a chance to complete the course, and offer encouragement. Each person should be timed and then, if possible, given a second chance to try to beat the first time. Talk about how it felt to complete the course and how you responded to the challenge. Was it exhilarating or terrifying? Did the encouragement you received make a difference?

NITZAVIM

Our Ancestors before Us

> "I make this covenant . . . not with you alone, but both with those who are standing here with us this day . . . and with those who are not with us here this day."
>
> (Deuteronomy 29:13-14)

Many of us approach life as if we were clean slates—as if, with some coaching and a few good books, we can be exactly who we wish to be. But that is not the whole story. We are influenced by the way we were brought up and by many factors outside our control, such as our health, socioeconomic status, and family members, that play a large role in our lives.

In this Torah portion, *Nitzavim*, Moses declares that God has made a covenant not only with the current generation, but with generations that came before and with future generations. Thus we are part of a long chain of links, connecting us backward and forward. It's not all about us and our own generation. Our lives depend on those who came before us, and we bear responsibility to those who come after us.

It's important to distinguish between what is out of our control and what is in our power to shape. For example, we may have been born Jewish, but what will we do with that Jewish identity? We may not have choice concerning who our family members are, but we do choose the relationships we forge with our extended family, our parents, and our siblings. It's up to us to choose what to pass on from all we have inherited.

—by Rabbi Dianne Cohler-Esses

MAKING CONNECTIONS

- What are some of the traits and talents you received from parents and grandparents?
- How do you plan to take advantage of these gifts you have received?
- Which of your personality traits and your abilities would you want your children to have?

Word collage/cloud

Make a collage or word cloud (which is essentially a collage of words) that describes you—your identity, interests, relationships, and values. Find and print pictures or words from online, or cut them from magazines. Assemble them into your collage or word cloud, making the most important words or images the largest and the less important ones smaller. Which ideas in your collage or word cloud did you inherit or receive without having chosen them, and which have you actively chosen?

Choose Life

Is smoking good for you? Most sane people will tell you that it's not, including people who themselves are smokers! Isn't it strange that we sometimes consciously make choices that are bad for us?

In this Torah portion, we are instructed by Moses to choose life. Why do we need to be instructed to do the obvious? The Torah recognizes that although we may very well know what is good for us and what is not, we still need to be reminded to make the right choices.

Overeating, using drugs, and smoking are all harmful activities. Yet countless people engage in them all the time. Even though we know that certain actions are dangerous, we do not always comprehend the long-term consequences of our actions. This Torah portion shows us that we need reminders to make proper choices. In each situation we confront, we can ask ourselves, "How can I choose life?"

—by Rabbi Moshe Becker

> "I have put before you life and death, blessing and curse."
> (Deuteronomy 30:19)

MAKING CONNECTIONS

- What are some reasons we do things that are bad for us?
- How can we learn to "choose life" when challenged?
- Talk about the slippery slope: what's wrong with just one cigarette, for example?

Guest speaker

Invite a recovering addict or alcoholic to speak about the disease of addiction and explain his or her recovery. Ask the speaker to relate to the topic "Choose Life."

Disobedience

> "They will forsake
> Me and break
> My covenant."
> (Deuteronomy 31:16)

Disobedience is an inevitable part of growing up. Children and teens test limits at times. What they are usually looking for is consistency in the way limits are set. When firm, appropriate boundaries are set, it's as if a safe container has been created that holds children secure in the knowledge that their parents care.

In this *parashah*, *Vayeilech*, God tells Moses that God's people will be disobedient and violate the covenant. Nevertheless, God keeps faith with the children of Israel and, despite their misbehavior, brings them into the Promised Land, flowing with milk and honey. God does not abandon God's people. Perhaps this is the oldest example of unconditional love.

Even though children test their parents, ideally parents and children remain connected to each other. Both parents and children change and grow and arrive at a new stage in their relationship. Relationships are a process, and we pray that parents and children have many years of evolving connection.

—*by Rabbi Dianne Cohler-Esses*

MAKING CONNECTIONS

- Do you remember when and why you have broken rules?
- Is it hard for you to live with rules? Why or why not?
- Which rules do you think are fair, and which are unfair?
- How do you react when rules are applied unevenly or inconsistently?

Freedom/responsibility timeline

Relationships between parents and children change and grow. Being a teen means gaining new freedoms and new responsibilities. Work in pairs to come up with a timeline of future freedoms and responsibilities. What are some upcoming freedoms you are looking forward to (such as getting a driver's license, traveling alone, and so on)? What are some responsibilities you will be taking on? Draw a timeline or chart showing exactly when you expect these new freedoms and responsibilities to be established.

Growth through Discomfort

You probably don't enjoy pain. Most people don't. You probably don't enjoy uncomfortable confrontations or difficult tasks either. It's easy enough to take a pill to alleviate pain, but we shouldn't be running from difficult situations. Instead, challenging situations should be seen for what they are: valuable growth opportunities.

Moses nears the end of his life. He is old and frail, but this does not stop him from making the most of his days. He uses his time to speak to his people and impart final words of guidance and wisdom. It isn't easy for him, but it is his last chance to impart his message.

Society has conditioned us to identify happiness with extreme comfort and the satisfaction of our material desires. Nobody likes pain, and we should certainly enjoy the world in which we live. But there's much more to life than comfort. To accomplish our goals takes effort. We must be willing to put ourselves out there when someone needs help and when confronting those whom we upset or who upset us. Challenges give us the opportunity to flex our "muscles" and take another step toward becoming the person we want to be.

—by Rabbi Moshe Becker

"Gather the people—
men, women, children
and the strangers in
your communities—
that they may hear
and so learn."

(Deuteronomy 31:12)

MAKING CONNECTIONS

- What makes you happy?
- What are some of your goals in life?
- Do you have role models who you know have pushed themselves through difficult situations?
- How does accomplishing your goal feel after working hard?

SMART goals

Learn about SMART goals (Specific, Measurable, Achievable, Relevant, and Timely). Work in pairs to each set one SMART goal for the next six months, and write down the steps you will need to take to achieve it.

Developing the Ability to Listen

HA'AZINU

"Give ear . . . let me speak . . . hear the words I utter."
(Deuteronomy 32:1)

What do we mean by listening? When people say, "Listen to me," they may mean "I want you to do something," "I want you to pay attention to what I am saying," or "I want you to take my suggestion and change your behavior." All of these different kinds of listening can be difficult. Sometimes we may not want to do what we are asked, or our attention may be elsewhere, or we may not want to change our behavior.

This Torah portion begins with the injunction to "give ear," to listen. It is filled with Moses's criticism of the children of Israel, criticism designed to make them into a better people. For the sake of the future of Israel, it is crucial that the children of Israel take Moses's words to heart.

We can all use practice in improving our listening. It can be easier to listen to others when we know that they will listen to us. We may be more available to take suggestions when we are given choices. When we have a sense of control, we are less likely to get into a power struggle. If we feel listened to and feel that we can shape our own environment, we are more likely to be open to suggestions from others. Learning to be better listeners continues to be important, even more so as distractions multiply. Listening is one of the most important skills we can practice and develop.

—*by Rabbi Dianne Cohler-Esses*

MAKING CONNECTIONS

- When is it hardest for you to listen?
- When is it easiest for you to listen?
- Why do you think listening is important?
- Can you listen and do other things at the same time (multitask)?

Listen and draw

You will need paper and colored pencils/markers. Prepare a one- to two-sentence description of a scene that includes at least seven different objects, five different colors, and a few different numbers of items. Ask your group to listen to the entire description and then draw what you described. After they finish, go back through the description and see who got all the items. Talk about how hard/easy this game was.

Facing Our Personal Monsters

> "But for fear of the taunts of the foe."
> (Deuteronomy 32:27)

No matter how old you are, you have probably dealt with your share of fears. Whether it's a fear of flying, public speaking, spiders—or a fear of monsters hiding under your bed—sometimes our rational self is overpowered by emotions. We cannot think logically, and fears take over. Yet, we each have a treasure trove of personal strengths, such as the ability to love, to solve problems, or to stay calm and organized. When monsters begin gathering under our beds, how can we tap into our strengths?

The children of Israel also had fears and moments of terror. They were afraid of their enemies and of being teased or judged by the larger nations. As they wandered in the wilderness, there were times when they lost hope and when they stopped believing in Moses and God. They forgot how to access their strengths.

Like the children of Israel, we have moments when we're overpowered by our fears. When these moments come, our greatest resources are our internal strengths. Often we need the support of our families to help us and to remind us that we're strong enough, brave enough, and smart enough to overcome the obstacles in our way. Together, we can learn how to face the spiders, the airplanes, and even the monsters under the beds.

—by Rabbi Yael Hammerman

MAKING CONNECTIONS

- What scares you, and why?
- What are your personal strengths?
- How can you use your strengths to overcome your fears?

Guided meditation

Sit quietly with your eyes closed. One person reads the following: Imagine you are about to enter a beautiful garden. Beside the garden gate is a river. This river carries away fears. Think of a fear you have. Hold it in your hands and feel it. Then gently place it in the water and watch it glide away. Do this for each fear you have [pause for two minutes]. When you have placed all your fears into the river, gently open the garden gate. Walk through this beautiful garden and smell each of the flowers [pause for three minutes]. When you are ready, open your eyes.

Ha'azinu

Self-Deception

"Children unworthy
of God—that crooked,
perverse generation."
(Deuteronomy 32:5)

Every so often we get caught, or catch ourselves, doing something wrong. We may come up with creative justifications for what we did. The person I snapped at was rude to me first. Or I stole a game because the store makes too much money anyway.

In this Torah portion, Moses reminds us that when we do things that are wrong, we must focus on the imperfection in ourselves and not use twisted logic to find something else to blame. Modern psychological studies show that all people think they are basically good, regardless of how bad their actions. That is because people judge themselves by their motives, not by their actions. Interestingly, the Book of Proverbs notes, "All of a person's ways are right in one's own eyes" (Proverbs 16:2).

There is no way to correct our bad actions if we do not see them as wrong. There are people in your life who have the ability to think clearly: parents, teachers, coaches, friends, siblings, or grandparents. Look to those in your life who exemplify "untwisted" thinking and objectivity. They are the ones to look up to and try to learn from.

—by Rabbi Moshe Becker

MAKING CONNECTIONS

- Why is it "twisted" to blame someone else for your mistakes?
- Suppose the other person really is wrong; why is it helpful to focus away from him or her and into yourself?
- Think of two older people you know who are wise and mature and who model clarity of thought.

Cheshbon hanefesh

It is a Jewish practice to take a *cheshbon hanefesh*, an "accounting of the soul," in the days leading up to Rosh Hashanah and Yom Kippur, the time of year when this Torah portion is read. Get a notebook and set aside at least twenty minutes to write about the past year or past week. Where have you succeeded? Where could you have done better? Are there people to whom you need to apologize? Are there people you need to forgive? If you want to, you can share this with a person you trust, or use it on your own to plan for how you would like to improve.

162

Counting Our Blessings

"This is the blessing
with which Moses
. . . bade the
Israelites farewell."

(Deuteronomy 33:1)

We all want to be successful and happy, but the road to success and happiness is sometimes mysterious. We may need to redefine success and happiness. For example, the basics such as having a family, a roof over our heads, enough to eat, and enjoyable tasks are all blessings we may enjoy right now. We may want more for ourselves than we have now, yet it's crucial for our own sense of happiness to be aware of and grateful for what we have right at this moment.

In this Torah portion, when Moses blesses the tribe of Zebulun and Issachar, he tells them to rejoice in their journeys and in their tents. In other words, whether they are on a path or at home, it's important to rejoice. We can learn from this that sometimes the journey is just as important as the end result.

The ability to rejoice is another blessing we can count in our lives. We all experience setbacks. Focusing on the positives rather than on the negatives, even though those negatives seem very important at the time, can foster better perspective and balance. The capacity to feel joy is tied directly to being able to enjoy the blessings we have, and joy is contagious. We can spread joy to others by appreciating our blessings.

—by Rabbi Dianne
Cohler-Esses

MAKING CONNECTIONS

- What do you think could make you happier in your life?
- Have you ever been very upset about a situation but, now in hindsight, you realize that it was a blessing in disguise?
- What are five blessings in your life for which you are thankful?

Gratitude flower

Use colored paper to make a flower with a circle at the center and petals around the circle. At the center put your name and/or the words "I'm grateful for." Write something you are grateful for on each petal. You can put everyone's flowers together for a "gratitude garden."

163

V'ZOT HAB'RACHAH

Your Living Will

> "Joshua . . . was filled with the spirit of wisdom because Moses had laid his hands upon him."
>
> (Deuteronomy 34:9)

We take pictures at happy occasions, and we make yearbooks. These are ways in which we try to remember events or experiences. Something in our psyche intuits that there is significance beyond the present moment. It's this drive that leads us to think about the mark we want to make in this world. Do we want to be remembered for being selfish or for fairness and kindness to all?

Torah portion *V'zot Hab'rachah* contains Moses's parting words, his last wishes to the Jewish nation. He gives blessings, instructions, and direction. He reminds them of their individual roles as tribes along with their collective mission as a nation. His job as a leader never ends, and near his death he continues to inspire.

Think about the messages by which you would like to be known. What instructions would you have for yourself, your family, and friends? Will your words be uplifting and motivating to yourself and others? We all keep developing, and we can have a profound impact on our world. How is it that we want to be known?

—by Rabbi Moshe Becker

MAKING CONNECTIONS

- What values would you want to be known by in life?
- What would you most want to avoid in life?
- How can you be of help to others by your actions?
- Why should you care what others think of you?

Learning about legacy

Choose a historical figure or ancestor you would like to learn more about. Find written materials or people to interview about the impact this person had on others. Write one paragraph about what you think this person's legacy is and what it means to you.

Subject Index

Subject Index continued from page 167

About the Writers and Editors

Fred Claar, Content Creator/Editor/Writer

Fred Claar is a retired business owner. He is currently a board member of the Jewish Education Project, My Jewish Learning, and Jewish Student Connection, as well as a member of a Commission on Jewish Identity and Renewal (COJIR) task force of UJA. Fred teaches Jewish issues and texts to high schoolers once a month and frequently teaches school groups from seventh grade through college about the Holocaust at the Museum of Jewish Heritage in New York City.

As a continuing student, Fred takes several Talmud or related courses annually. Previously, around 1980, Fred created a successful Judaic family program built around the weekly Torah portion for the National Young Leadership Cabinet of UJA and was the patron of BJE's "Around the Shabbat Table" from 2003 to 2007. Fred is a 1963 graduate of Tufts University, where he met his wife of over fifty years, Joyce. They live in Westchester, New York, near their children and grandchildren.

Joyce Claar, Advisor/Editor

Joyce Claar was an English and special education teacher in high school and middle school for sixteen years and maintained a private tutoring practice. For the next twenty years, she taught adult classes for the high school equivalency (GED), on workplace literacy, and on basic skills for nursing, retiring in 2008. In 2001, she was chosen as Teacher of the Year in Workforce Preparation by NYAACE, a professional educational organization.

For many years Joyce chaired her synagogue's Social Action Committee, served on the Synagogue 2000 team, and was a weekly visitor to a disabled homebound woman for ten years through Dorot's Friendly Visitor program. She is a member of the Executive Committee and Board of Directors of the Westchester Jewish Council and the former chairperson of Westchester Adult Jewish Education (WAJE).

Rabbi Moshe Becker, Writer

Rabbi Moshe Becker writes and lectures extensively on Jewish law, history, and philosophy. He co-founded the Jewish Renaissance Experience, an innovative Jewish education program in Westchester County, New York. Rabbi Becker lives in New York with his family and is an executive at the New York City Department of Education.

Rabbi Dianne Cohler-Esses, Writer

Rabbi Dianne Cohler-Esses is the first Syrian Jewish woman to be ordained as a rabbi. She was ordained in 1995 at the Jewish Theological Seminary. She is currently a freelance educator and writer, teaching and writing about a wide range of Jewish subjects, and the director of lifelong learning at Romemu in New York City. She lives in New York with her journalist husband and their three children.

Rabbi Gail Diamond, Editor/Activities Creator

Rabbi Gail Diamond was ordained in 1993 from Reconstructionist Rabbinical College. She served as a pulpit rabbi in Attleboro, Massachusetts, before making *aliyah* in 2001. She was associate director of the Conservative Yeshiva in Jerusalem, where she taught for fourteen years. Since 2015, she has been a freelance translator, editor, and writer, focusing on education and sociology. She lives in Tzur Hadassah with her family, where she is part of Reform, modern Orthodox, and partnership religious communities.

Rabbi Judith Greenberg, Writer
Rabbi Judith Greenberg was ordained as a rabbi at the Jewish Theological Seminary in 2013, where she also received a master's degree in Midrash. Judy teaches Talmud, Bible, Midrash, and *t'filah* at Rochelle Zell Jewish High School in the Chicago suburbs. She lives in Evanston with her family.

Rabbi Yael Hammerman, Writer
Ordained by the Jewish Theological Seminary of America, Rabbi Yael Hammerman also received a degree from its Davidson Graduate School of Jewish Education. Before joining Ansche Chesed in Toms River, New Jersey, as director of congregational learning, she was a student rabbi at Congregation Eitz Chaim in Monroe, New York, and director of student placement at the Jewish Theological Seminary's rabbinical and cantorial schools. Rabbi Hammerman lives in New York City with her husband, Rabbi Josh Rabin, and their daughter, Hannah.

Lois Kohn-Claar, Advisor/Editor
After years of working in the field of education and educational technology, Lois now devotes herself to Jewish communal service and philanthropy. She is the past chair of UJA-Federation of NY/Westchester Women and has served on the Board of Directors of UJA-Federation NY as well as several committees. Lois is a Wexner Heritage Graduate and a founding member of the Neshamot Women's Impact Philanthropy group. She serves on the Board of Directors and Executive Committee of the Jewish Education Project, Foundation for Jewish Camp Board of Trustees, BBYO International Board of Directors, Schechter Westchester Board of Trustees, Penn Hillel National Board of Governors, and the University of Pennsylvania's Graduate School of Education Board of Overseers. She holds a BA and MS in education from the University of Pennsylvania.

Rabbi Kerrith Rosenbaum, Writer
Rabbi Kerrith Rosenbaum is currently the director of education at Adas Israel in Washington, DC. She previously worked at Tufts University Hillel, Congregation B'nai Jeshurun, and UJA-Federation of New York. She participated in the Hartman-Hillel iEngage Fellowship for Campus Leaders and the Senior Educators Cohort of M²: The Institute for Experiential Jewish Education.

Rabbi Charles E. Savenor, Writer
Rabbi Charles E. Savenor serves as the director of congregational education at Park Avenue Synagogue in New York. Previously he was director of *kehilla* (congregational) enrichment for the United Synagogue of Conservative Judaism (USCJ) and led USCJ's Family Israel Experience. His articles have appeared in *Hadassah Magazine*, *Jewish Week*, eJewish Philanthropy, and *CJ Magazine*. Rabbi Savenor blogs on parenting at www.familyinorbit.com and www.kveller.com. In addition, he serves as a volunteer fund-raiser for lone soldiers in the Israeli Defense Forces.

Acknowledgments

I want to recognize individuals and resources that have contributed to my love of the timeliness and relevance of our Jewish texts.

Initially in my early thirties, I was lucky to be influenced by Rabbi Shlomo Riskin, who opened my eyes to the value and relevance of the Torah to twentieth-century life. My second teacher was Rabbi Yitz Greenberg, who deepened my knowledge of Jewish history and theology. Rabbi Herb Friedman, whom I met as a member of the National Young Leadership Cabinet of UJA, also contributed to my appreciation of Jewish texts.

During my adult years, I have studied with many rabbis and regularly read writings of many others who have given me much joy of learning. All of them continued to reinforce the current importance and value of the messages in our ancient texts.

Dennis Prager's practicality for growing observance and the rationality in his positions have been a strong influence through the years. Rabbi Lord Jonathan Sacks impresses me with his explanations, positions, and reasoning.

Locally, I want to mention Rabbi Alfredo Borodowski, an outstanding teacher and spiritual force from the pulpit. Rabbi Adin Steinsaltz first excited me about the relevance of the Talmud to all aspects of modern life. Studying with Rabbi Yaakov Bienenfeld has expanded my understanding and appreciation for the Talmud.

My first rabbi, Jacob Goldberg, inspired awe and reverence for Judaism. He and his brother-in-law, Rabbi Herman Rosenwasser, were important influences on my spiritual development.

Most of all, I want to single out my parents and grandparents. My mother and father had wonderful Jewish feelings that were contagious. Grandpa Jacob Patent exposed me to his adult learning and a whole world of worship that is my earliest and deepest memory of the positive power of Judaism on modern life. Grandpa Shlomo Fischel Claar (Claar is a typo at Ellis Island 115 years ago) died when my father was six years old. Grandpa Claar was a graduate of the Lodz Yeshiva and might be proud of the Jewish development of some of his grandchildren.

Any comments about my Jewish spiritual growth must include my wife, Joyce, for almost fifty-four years and hopefully many more years to come. Joyce came to me with a strong Conservative background. Joyce has been by my side encouraging, tolerating, and delighting in my adult Jewish enlightenment.

Almost forty-five years ago, Rabbi Peter Rubenstein led Joyce and me to decide to emphasize Shabbat with our family. The positive impact of that decision has been a most significant event in our lives and is the distant fore-runner of the creation of Values and Ethics.

In the beginning of this project, it was my good fortune to engage Rabbi Dianne Cohler-Esses as a part-time writer. She deftly translated my ideas from outline form into her beautiful prose style.

I am especially grateful to Daniel Septimus, the former editor-in-chief of My Jewish Learning and now the executive director of the innovative Jewish learning site Sefaria. Daniel recognized value in our simplified and inclusive approach to show relevance in each Torah portion. He began to feature our work in 2010 on his very fast-growing website My Jewish Learning. This opportunity pushed me to produce lessons more rapidly.

Soon after we were established on My Jewish Learning, I opened our original website, called Torah Topics for Today, with the help of Jill Nastasia, who began our theme concept. Shortly thereafter I was contacted by Behrman House to get some of our lessons on their newly developing Online Learning Center. Under time pressure to produce original material rapidly, I needed help in writing up my concepts in the consistent formula that made us successful. I reached out to the Jewish Theological Seminary, where I was fortunate to begin working with senior rabbinical students, now Rabbis Judith Greenberg, Yael Hammerman, and Kerrith Rosenbaum. Rabbi Moshe Becker, a teacher and friend, helped with completing our body of work and was joined by an accomplished blogger, creative educator, and friend, Rabbi Charles E. Savenor.

Dan Oehlsen upgraded our second website and effectively helped me complete the initial publishing of our book. Our highly competent, accomplished, and very busy daughter-in-law, Lois Kohn-Claar, originally helped by editing as her time allowed and continued as an encourager, idea source, and promoter of our collaborative work.

Behrman House's involvement has improved our work by broadening our focus to include teachers along with parents, asking me to provide Torah portion quotes, and employing Rabbi Gail Diamond to edit the manuscript and design meaningful activities for each page. Dena Neusner, executive editor of Behrman House, has been a professional watchful eye and positive influence on the improvements to Values and Ethics: Torah Topics for Today. I am grateful to David Behrman and his team for recognizing the value of our work and publishing this improved version.

To all of the writers and teachers who have educated and influenced my adult Jewish journey, I am grateful that our paths crossed. I am a much better person from their teachings, which have eventually become part of who I am.

Fred S. Claar

Sources

Below are sources I have learned much from and may have used to select some ideas developed in *Values and Ethics*.

Goldin, Shmuel. *Unlocking the Torah Text*. New York: Gefen, 2014.

Hammer, Rabbi Reuven. *Entering Torah*. Jerusalem: Gefen, 2009.

Leibowitz, Nehama. *Studies in Bereshit, Shemot, Vayikra, Bamidbar, and Devarim*. Jerusalem: The Joint Authority for Jewish Zionist Education, 1993.

Loeb, Sorel G., and Barbara B. Kadden. *Teaching Torah*. Denver, CO: A.R.E., 1997.

Menken, Rabbi Yaakov. *The Everything Torah Book*. Avon, MA: Adams Media, 2005.

Rabbinical Assembly, United Synagogue of Conservative Judaism. *Etz Hayim: Torah and Commentary*. Philadelphia: Jewish Publication Society, 1985.

Sacks, Rabbi Jonathan. *Covenant and Conversation*. New Milford, CT: Maggid Books, 2015.

Scheinbaum, Rabbi A. L. *Peninim on the Torah*. Cleveland Heights, OH: Peninim, 2015.

Twerski, Rabbi Abraham J. *Twerski on Chumash*. Brooklyn: Shaar Press, 2003.

Weissblum, Moshe P. *Table Talk*. New York: Jonathan David, 2005.

The Calm-Down Sandwich activity on page 82 (Reason Gets Lost in Anger) was developed by Barbara Gruener and accessed at http://corneroncharacter.blogspot.co.il/2012/08/strategy-sandwiches.html, used by permission.

The Gratitude Flower activity on page 163 (Counting Our Blessings) was developed by Momentous Institute and accessed at http://momentousinstitute.org/blog/gratitude-garden, used by permission.

The publisher gratefully acknowledges the following sources of photographs and graphic images:

Shutterstock: Olivier Le Moal (front cover compass), Chris Parypa Photography (front cover Torah text), adike (back cover, iv), Szefei 8, Bigbubblebee99 15, Kryzhov 42, Donna Ellen Coleman 59, ChiccoDodiFC 64, Pathdoc 83, Bina k 88, Anekoho 108, Mimagephotography 111, VGstockstudio 119, Monkey Business Images 127, Golden Pixels LLC 130, Wavebreakmedia 146, Fongbeerredhot 157, Sergey Nivens 161.

Thinkstock/ iStock: loooby 4, OcusFocus 5, Elenathewise 6, welcomia 7, soleg 9, IuriiSokolov 10, fuse 11, Chiociolla 18, shironosov 19, Olga_Danylenko 20, Rawpixel 22, monkeybusinessimages 23, mtreasure 24, Ig0rZh 25, asafta 27, veronicagomepola 28, VladimirFLoyd 31, double_p 32, cdoughboy2000 33, LuckyBusiness 34, monkeybusinessimages 35, michaeljung 36, alexis84 37, Srdjana1 40, robeo 41, LyubovKobyakova 44, bwancho 46, justinkendra 47, AlexStepanov 48, Tomwang112 49, monkeybusinessimages 50, yelo34 51, IPGGutenbergUKLtd 52, pbcpa 53, deymos 55, MrPants 57, lisafx 60, AVAVA 61, joyfnp 62, c8501089 63, michaeljung 65, VladyslavDanilin 66, igabriela 67, nautiluz56 69, JOHNGOMEZPIX 70, monkeybusinessimages 74, lisafx 75, draganajokmanovic 76, George Doyle 77, DenKuvaiev 78, sergeyryzhov 80, jacoblund 81, JackF 82, JackF 85, JohanJK 86, keeweeboy 87, dolgachov 89, panco971 91, xavigm 92, m-gucci 94, karelnoppe 95, bowdenimages 103, a-wrangler 105, Viktor_Gladkov 106, spwidoff 107, ChristinLola 109, GMint 110, doble-d 112, shironosov 113, akpakp 114, JackF 115, doble-d 117, Nesho 118, DenKuvaiev 120, katelig 121, wihteorchid 122, Halfpoint 124, iVangelos 126, loooby 128, ABedov 135, rejeanperreault 136, ImageegamI 139, gmast3r 140, stacey_newman 141, Anna_Om 144, monkeybusinessimages 145, SurkovDimitri 147, Meinzahn 148, Martinan 149, monkeybusinessimages 152, veronicagomepola 153, dnaveh 156, JackF 158, JochenSchoenfeld 159, monkeybusinessimages 160, dobokiStock 162, Goodluz 163, Halfpoint 164.

Thinkstock: Pixland/ Pixland v, Jupiterimages/ liquidlibrary 2, Jupiterimages, Brand X Pictures/ Stockbyte 3, Digital Vision/ Photodisc 12, Wavebreakmedia Ltd/ Wavebreak Media 13, Jupiterimages/ Stockbyte 14, Purestock/ Purestock 16, Jupiterimages/ BananaStock 17, Ingram Publishing/ Ingram Publishing 21, Photodisc/ Photodisc 26, Visual Ideas/Nora Pelaez/ Blend Images 29, Yuri Arcurs/ Hemera 30, BananaStock 43, Mike Powell/ DigitalVision 45, Comstock/ Stockbyte 54, altrendo images/ Stockbyte 56, Wavebreakmedia Ltd/ Wavebreak Media 58, Ingram Publishing/ Ingram Publishing 68, Jupiterimages/ Stockbyte 71, Jupiterimages/ PHOTOS.com 79, Ingram Publishing/ Ingram Publishing 84, Chris Amaral/ DigitalVision 90, John Howard/ DigitalVision 93, Comstock Images/ Stockbyte 96, BananaStock 97, BananaStock 98, Jupiterimages/ Pixland 99, Jose Luis Pelaez Inc/ Blend Images 102, Anna Dudko/ Hemera 104, Digital Vision/ DigitalVision 116, Jupiterimages/ PHOTOS.com 123, Photos.com/ PHOTOS.com 125, Stockbyte/ Stockbyte 129, Pixland/ Pixland 134, Anthony Harris/ Hemera 137, Image Source Pink/ Image Source 138, Andrew Olney/ DigitalVision 142, Brand X Pictures/ Stockbyte 143, Jupiterimages/ Pixland 150, John Howard/ DigitalVision 151, Ernest Prim/ Hemera 154, Pixland/ Pixland 155.

Notes